Rome and the Literature of Gardens

CLASSICAL INTER/FACES

Series editors: Susanna Braund and Paul Cartledge

ROME AND THE LITERATURE OF GARDENS

Victoria Emma Pagán

Duckworth

First published in 2006 by
Gerald Duckworth & Co. Ltd.
90-93 Cowcross Street, London EC1M 6BF
Tel: 020 7490 7300
Fax: 020 7490 0080
inquiries@duckworth-publishers.co.uk
www.ducknet.co.uk

A catalogue record for this book is available
from the British Library

ISBN-10: 0 7156 3506 9
ISBN-13: 9780715635063

Typeset by Ray Davies
Printed and bound in Great Britain by
MPG Books Ltd, Bodmin, Cornwall

Contents

For Abe and Ellie
inch by inch

Preface

Gardens are always for *next* year.
                                        Ian Hamilton Finlay

I aim this book at as wide an audience as possible. As a result, I deploy minimal in-text citations that manifest my debt to previous scholarship on gardens and garden literature; author's last name, year, and page number(s) if necessary, direct the reader to further discussion and sometimes disagreement. Translations are mostly my own, but occasionally I borrow or adapt from a predecessor. The titles of Latin works are nearly all translated into English; Greek is transliterated.

Each chapter opens with an 'unconnected' sentence on gardening by the late Ian Hamilton Finlay (1925-2006), a concrete poet and landscape artist recognized as 'one of the most critically respected contemporary Scottish artists' (Patrizio 1999, 58). His sculptures adorn gardens at the Max Planck Institute, Stuttgart (1975), Stockwood Park, Luton (1991), The Schloßpark, Grevenbroich, near Dusseldorf (1995), the Serpentine Gallery, Hyde Park, London (1998), and St George's Brandon Hill, Bristol (2000) (Eyres 2000, 152-3). His work draws on themes from classical literature and philosophy, in what Eyres calls a 'polemological neo-classicism' (2000, 164). Perhaps his most significant work is Little Sparta, a four-acre garden in Dunsyre, Scotland (Bann 1981 and Sheeler 2003 are the most detailed introductions).

Born in Nassau, Bahamas, in 1925, Finlay was raised in Scotland. He served in the army during World War II. His first works, short stories, were published in 1958. In 1961, he founded the Wild Hawthorn Press, which until 1967 published twenty-five issues of the periodical *Poor.Old.Tired.Horse*; contributors included e.e. cummings, Pablo Neruda, Günter Grass, Paul Celan, and Herman Hesse. In 1966, Finlay moved to Dunsyre and began work transforming a 'desolate spot' (Abrioux 1985, 12) known as Stonypath into a world-famous garden.

In 1978, Finlay began his 'Five Year Hellenization Plan', for the garden at Stonypath, which he renamed 'Little Sparta', in opposition to Edinburgh's proclaimed title as the 'Athens of the North' (Eyres 2006, 22). He transformed a simple agricultural building in the farm courtyard into a gallery, and finally into a Temple to Apollo, sowing the seeds for what was to become the Little Spartan War, a long running dispute with the local regional authority over the status of the garden. Finlay maintained that the Temple to Apollo was a religious, not a secular site, and so it qualified for the normal rates exemption accorded to religious buildings. In 1983, sheriffs attempted to seize works from the Temple, and a Strathclyde officer returned and succeeded in removing several works (Sheeler 2003, 17). After closing for a time, the garden reopened in 1984 and is open to visitors today.

Nature constantly threatens to reclaim Finlay's garden and its artifacts (some 275 works of art). In 1994, the Little Sparta Trust was formed, whose objective is 'to maintain the garden to the high standard the artist has set, and to secure the long-term future of the garden and its treasures' (see www.littlesparta.co.uk). Eyres (2006) sets forth just some of the logistical problems that confront the conservation of this fragile work of art, including financial security, accommodation for large numbers of visitors, and the training of future gardeners. It is likely that the garden will survive best in visual media, in what John Dixon Hunt calls the 'afterlife' of gardens.

As for the epigraphs to my chapters, Finlay issued several series of 'unconnected' or 'detached' sentences on gardening, following the model of William Shenstone's 1764 essay, 'Unconnected Thoughts on Gardening' (Scobie 1995, 195). These aphoristic *sententiae* demonstrate Finlay's insistence on the power of individual sentences as against connected prose (Morgan 1995, 138), as Finlay himself so succinctly states: 'Consecutive sentences are the beginning of the secular.' Both Shenstone and Finlay in their 'unconnected' ways, suggest to me a kind of disparity in conceptual analysis and an engagement in the rhetoric of the garden that calls for disconnected, disjointed, antithetical prose. Although they force a strong sense of disconnect, nevertheless these *sententiae* dissolve pretence and disclose the fundamental principles of the garden. They are not cryptic or inscrutable; on the contrary, they purport to lay bare the garden, even as they invite debate. Finlay manages to make stereotype (a mode of discourse that hovers perilously close to prejudice) provocative.

Unconnected – detached sentences are by necessity scattered and dispersed. Some that were painted onto the gallery walls at Inverleith House, in the heart of the Royal Botanic Garden, are reproduced by Eyres (2006, 27). Still others can be found in Abrioux (1985, 38). I found the *Detached Sentences* for the Introduction and Chapters 1-5 in Gillanders (1998, no page numbers) who records two dozen aphorisms. The unconnected sentence for the Preface is from Scobie (1995, 196).

In April 2000, Eleanor Windsor Leach hosted a small conference at Indiana University, where the idea for this book was planted; I thank her for the invitation to participate. Initial research for this project was generously funded by a Career Enhancement Fellowship from the Woodrow Wilson National Fellowship Foundation for the year 2002-3. Further financial support from the American Association of University Women in the Summer 2004 guaranteed its timely completion. In the final stages, I travelled to the Dumbarton Oaks Research Library and Collection in Washington, DC; I would like to thank Sheila Klos, Curator of the Garden and Landscape Studies collection for her assistance, and John and Michele Pagán for their hospitality. I am grateful to Jessie Sheeler of the Little Sparta Trust for facilitating my visit to Little Sparta in Dunsyre, Scotland. Thanks, then, to the University of Florida for providing funding for both expeditions.

To W.R. Johnson, whose *Lucretius and the Modern World* inaugurated this series, I extend heartfelt gratitude for teaching me how to think about literature. I warmly acknowledge the editors of this inspired series: Deborah Blake for her patience, Paul Cartledge for suggesting I include Augustine's conversion, and Susanna Braund for her unflinching support and her steadfast friendship. Tim Johnson deserves special mention for his careful reading of the chapter on Horace; countless other colleagues, as well as students, research assistants, librarians, friends, and family are unnamed but not unappreciated. Such support will be evident on every page.

My greatest debt is to my husband Andrew Wolpert, who alone tended the garden behind our old house in Madison, complete with a patch of basil that kept us in pesto all summer and a parade of flowers from March to August – no mean feat in that begrudging Wisconsin climate. In Florida, the rewards of his labour are year-round, and spectacular. My mother used to say, 'You kids are growing like weeds!' In the last six years since this book was contracted, I witnessed this phenomenon first-hand. Children grow as fast as weeds, and certainly faster than slender paperbacks. Therefore, I dedicate *Rome and the Literature of Gardens* to Abraham Ricardo and Natalie Eleutheria, on the eve of Kindergarten, with the modest hope that should they someday read it, they may not mind that I was sometimes some place else.

Introduction

Sites of Contest

Certain gardens are described as retreats when they
are really attacks.

Ian Hamilton Finlay

I

A garden is a physical experience that can engage the senses of sight,
smell, hearing, touch, and taste. Separated from the rest of the landscape by a clearly defined boundary, a garden maintains both form
and function by means of scrupulous upkeep. Within its borders,
pruning stops transgressive growth so as to ensure a proper aesthetic
balance as well as a fruitful harvest. Yet the continuous process of
growth and decay transforms a garden, rendering it a dynamic space,
sometimes bursting forth in exuberant colour, other times withering
and fading. This cyclical process gives the impression of permanence.
Yet the ever changing appearance of a garden and its dependence on
the vagaries of the weather destabilize it and imbue it with a sense of
random chance (Ross 1998, 9).

Fast behind the word garden follows 'Eden', in turn evoking paradise. Because a garden requires such arduous labour that is
nevertheless at the mercy of certain uncontrollable elements, an ideal
garden, sustained by divine power, holds out a promise of a better life;
this 'paradise' figures in a variety of ancient religions across the
ancient Mediterranean (Carroll 2003, 122-33). The garden is also a
spiritual, non-corporeal experience, endowed with mythological, religious, social, socio-economic, and even intellectual and philosophical
meanings. These meanings are bestowed upon a garden by the range
of human activities that take place in it: work and leisure, decorum
and licence, retreat and pursuit, rituals both sacred and profane. 'A
central feature of our enjoyment of gardens,' according to garden
philosopher Stephanie Ross, 'is imagining ourselves performing some
sort of action in that landscape, or in response to it, coupled with the

1

possibility of actually going on and doing one or all of these things' (Ross 1998, 166). Any garden thus has two manifestations, the physical and the metaphysical. Or, as Ross puts it, 'gardens are at once parts of the real world – actual pieces of land – and also virtual worlds – coherent sets of possible sensory stimuli' (Ross 1998, 176). Already what appears to be a readily comprehended cultural artifact is really quite a complex space. This complexity is compounded when the garden is represented – and manipulated – in works of literature.

My subject is the garden as an expression of culture and society in Roman literature. For such an investigation, one would typically consult the agricultural treatises of Cato the Elder (234-149 BCE), Varro (116-27 BCE), Columella (writing around 60-5 CE), and Palladius (late fourth century CE), the *Georgics* of Vergil (70-19 BCE), the encyclopaedic *Natural History* of Pliny the Elder (23-79 CE), or the detailed descriptions of gardens in the letters of Pliny the Younger (approximately 62-113 CE), for example. Technically, only Columella and Palladius write specifically at any length about gardens per se. For Cato and Varro, the garden is a tangential and ancillary subcategory of the larger enterprise of agriculture, and Vergil, as we shall see, declines to write about the garden altogether. I shall not ignore these valuable sources; however, to understand how the garden permeated Roman thought, I believe it is more fruitful to explore the representation of the garden across genres. When an author mentions gardens, whether in a technical treatise (as with Cato, Varro, Columella, and Palladius), a poem (as with Vergil), or in passing (as with the Elder and Younger Pliny), he adheres to certain literary conventions and is bound by didactic prescriptions. He must teach the reader how, where, and when certain plants are grown. But what happens when the garden becomes a setting and a background for other types of literary expressions, with other purposes? How does the garden, with all of its physical and metaphysical meanings, shape the ideological import of a work of literature?

To answer these questions, I have chosen to examine closely four seemingly disparate works of Roman literature. The first choice is obvious enough: Columella's hexameter poem on the garden. From this Neronian poem, I move back in time to Horace's *Satire* 1.8, a poem written about the newly created Gardens of Maecenas in Rome. These two works embrace the temporal spectrum of the Julio-Claudian dynasty; *Satire* 1.8 was written during the formative years of what was to become Augustus' regime (during the so-called triumviral period, 44-31 BCE), Columella's poem at the end, in the last days of the emperor Nero. Columella and Horace also give us representations of gardens both general and particular, the one describing how to cultivate a garden in broad terms, the other describing a specific garden. Furthermore, the gardens in these two poems exemplify the two extremes of Roman gardens, on the one hand, the small private gardens that yield produce for individuals, and on the other hand, the grand pleasure gardens owned by the wealthy and intended for public use.

My third and fourth texts are prose selections that balance the picture presented by the two poems above and likewise complement each other. In Tacitus' *Annals* Book 11 and in Augustine's *Confessions* Book 8, gardens are settings for events of extreme transgression and transformation. Tacitus relates how Messalina, wife of the emperor Claudius, is killed in the Gardens of Lucullus; Augustine describes his momentous conversion to Christianity in a garden in Milan. Again we see representations of both the grand public and small private garden. Tacitus composed the *Annals*, roughly speaking, between the years 110 and 117 CE; Augustine began his *Confessions* in the year 397 CE. These two works, together with the poems of Columella and Horace, allow us to see a deeply conservative perception of the garden that does not undergo significant change in the course of more than four hundred years. Even the advent of Christianity, with all of the social, economic, and political changes that it brings, does not effectively change the physical form and function of the garden; if anything, we shall see that in Augustine's representation, Christianity distils the essential metaphysics of the garden.

Finally, all four selections are taken from genres that are arguably uniquely Roman. Columella's agricultural treatise stands in a long line of Roman technical works on rhetoric, education, law, geography, aqueducts, and military strategy. Legend has it that the Romans invented satire; Greeks eschewed for the most part the annalistic format of history writing that Tacitus perfected; Augustine is credited by most as the inventor of autobiography in the western tradition (on the inception of autobiography in Republican Rome, see Chassignet 2003). Furthermore, Augustine may have been educated in the Greek language, but he admits outright to being a poor student. His inability to read Greek meant that its influence on his thought was always limited. The latest pronouncement is swift and decisive: 'A word on Augustine's Greek: pathetic' (O'Donnell 2005, 126). Thus, with these four texts, we are looking at distinctly Roman forms of expression.

Objections to my choices are serious enough to warrant elaboration. First, it goes without saying that all of these texts represent élite male notions of the garden; even sources that may convey something of the common man's experience of the garden were written by, and for, a literate élite. Women, when they appear in our texts, are constructed along certain principles that tell us more about male discourse on gardens than about women's lived experience in them. Secondly, my approach implies that the other unstudied gardens are variations of the gardens explored here, which are emblematic of gardens in the Roman literary imagination. My point is to suggest that the garden is a powerful locus of transgression and transformation throughout the long duration of classical Roman literature.

The selection of Columella, Horace, Tacitus, and Augustine means that other authors have been excluded; I say nothing of gardens in Lucretius or Statius, for example. I do not examine the *Georgics* or even the *Eclogues* of Vergil on their own terms, but in relation to the other texts. Most notably, I do not engage with the Greek predecessors (such as they are) to these four works of literature, preferring to take the Romans on their own terms. It would be reckless to deny the inescapable debt of Latin literature to Greek literature. No doubt the Greeks farmed and gardened and wrote about these activities, yet there is scant archaeological evidence, and literary references to gardens and gardening are infrequent. Although Varro catalogues over fifty Greek treatises on agriculture, no ancient treatise devoted specifically to gardening survives, or is even known, from classical Greece. Osborne performed an admirable service when, from these meagre sources, he assembled a composite picture of gardens in classical Greece (Osborne 1992; see also Carroll-Spillecke 1992). But the fact remains that not only are the material and literary remains from Roman gardens more copious than the Greek, but even the most general differences in geography and climate between the verdant Italian peninsula and the arid Greek landscape validate the decision to focus solely on Roman gardens, in Roman literature, as products of a Roman imagination.

4

Introduction

More unusual, and perhaps controversial, than my exclusions, are the inclusions throughout this book of references to modern works of literature, for example, a poem by Carolyn Forché and a novel by Nobel laureate J.M. Coetzee. (To the extent that gardens are predicated on exclusion and inclusion, 'closing-out' and 'closing-in', any book reproduces and reinscribes the essential principles of the garden on the literary imagination.) Most provocative will be the conclusion – the 'closing together' – of the book with a discussion of two plays by Tom Stoppard, who, together with Forché and Coetzee, reflects primarily the ambience of the modern world. The objection is patent: the historical conditions are far too different to make juxtaposition of ancient and modern worthwhile. Yet in their assumptions of what is a plausible and credible representation of a garden, as too in their depictions of psychological response to the effects of the garden, these modern works also reflect aspects of the contemporary literary imagination that can provide valuable comparanda. Simply put, by including modern works of literature I take responsibility for my own historical self-consciousness. For me, the garden is an 'invitation to explore and renegotiate the self against culture', which is, in the words of Pearcy, 'to take part in shared forms of human life and in shared discourse about what it means to be human' (2005, 132). The garden is but one approach to this formidable task.

Like so many gardens of the ancient Roman world, the gardens described by Columella, Horace, Tacitus, and Augustine no longer exist for us to visit. The designers, architects, patrons, the landscapes, the plant materials, the walls and pathways alike are all gone. In the absence of primary visual sources, such as plans, descriptions, and maps, and without a substantial corpus of archaeological finds, literature emerges as a valuable secondary source. As gardens are a way of being in the world, so literature about gardens is a way of articulating that existence. The time and space of actual gardens of the ancient city of Rome are lost; even when standing on the Palatine today, one experiences only ruins and reconstructions. The gardens of ancient Rome thus come to us in always already interpreted forms. The gardens in Roman literature are art forms recast in poetry and prose. My endeavour may be compared to studying sculpture by reading verbal descriptions of statues alone. Yet, far from sterile analysis, such a method allows us to see how gardens, deeply paradoxical

5

phenomena, shaped the thoughts of the authors who wrote about them. The pictures of gardens given by Columella, Horace, Tacitus, and Augustine not only make palpable a visual experience, they also generate and deploy a set of expectations about the viewing and experiencing of gardens. As we shall see, gardens bring other contradictions into high relief; however, before proceeding to the metaphysical abstractions of what gardens mean, let us lay a foundation of what we know about the physical aspects of Roman gardens.

II

A garden is a three-dimensional space within a clearly defined boundary, whose foundation is soil, in which plants are deliberately cultivated for the purpose of providing food or aesthetic pleasure. The varieties of cultivars are limitless. Likewise the aesthetic purpose is broadly conceived, so as to include such inorganic creations as Isamu Noguchi's Beinecke Courtyard at Yale University or such minimalist concepts as Alan Sonfist's 1973 *Seed Catcher*, a twenty-five-foot diameter circle of earth surrounded by stones in the middle of a chemical waste-ground. In 2005, artist-architect Lauren Bon installed 'Not A Cornfield', a living sculpture in the form of a field of corn – in downtown Los Angeles – complete with its own website (www.notacornfield.com) that carries a live webcam and audio stream, thereby digitizing and broadcasting the agricultural experience (and which, by the time this reaches publication, will likely be trashed from cyberspace, thereby recapitulating the garden's essential ephemerality). 'Garden' is also a verb, denoting an activity undertaken by human beings in nearly every climate, in nearly every age. Because gardening is a universal activity practised by nearly all cultures to some degree, it is a central, essential expression of a culture and a society. A garden is the way a particular people satisfies the physical need for food as well as the metaphysical need for beauty. Attention to the way the ancient Romans satisfied these needs sheds light on their cultural and social practices.

In the first place, the garden and the act of gardening were perceived by the Romans as just one facet of the larger project of agriculture. When Cato the Elder wrote his manual on farming, he prioritized the components of the ideal estate: first, a vineyard; second, a well-watered garden; third, an osier-bed; fourth, an olive yard; fifth, a meadow; sixth, a field of grain; seventh, a wood lot; eighth, an orchard; ninth, a grove of nut trees (Cato, *On Agriculture* 1.7). Likewise for Varro, the garden is a small part of the larger farm, meant to provide flowers or food, as the farmer wants or needs (*On Agriculture* 1.23.4). Vergil, as we shall see, omitted the garden altogether from his agricultural poem, the *Georgics* (4.147-8), while Columella made gardens the subject of a separate book within his agricultural treatise. On the Roman farm, the garden was a separate plot. In Roman agricultural treatises, gardens are separate topics. Both physically and in the literature, Roman gardens are extra-ordinary exceptions, set apart from the rest of the landscape and context.

Most of the material evidence for Roman gardens comes from the excavations at Pompeii, the city on the Bay of Naples that was destroyed by the eruption of Mount Vesuvius in 79 CE. The unusual circumstances of Pompeii have preserved more evidence about gardens than anywhere else on the Italian peninsula. As a result, much of what we know about Roman gardens derives from this one specific site. Yet, the information derived from Pompeii can be used as a starting point from which to draw inferences about other regions of Italy. In her monumental study of Pompeian gardens and her edited volume on the natural history of Pompeii, Jashemski (1979; 2002) combs through every square inch of gardens in the city. In contrast to her specialized work centred on Pompeii, Bowe (2004) takes a more general approach. He not only surveys gardens throughout the Roman world, spanning the provinces from the eastern empire to Britain, but also considers the influence of Roman gardens across the ages, from Byzantium to the twentieth century. Together, both scholars demonstrate that gardens were attached to private homes, public spaces, and shops and inns. The garden was an integral feature of domestic and public architecture, and a place for work, leisure, business, and religious worship.

Usually used in the singular, *hortus* often refers to a small vegetable plot adjacent to the kitchen; Farrar (1998, 16) locates this type of *hortus* in the back of the house. According to Huxley's account of the history of gardening, the Romans were the first to develop gardens as essential extensions to their houses (Huxley 1978, 31). Ideally, the mother of each family kept a garden for produce as well as flowers for

7

the household altars. Even town houses located within urban areas had a garden. The peristyle garden, located in the middle of the house, was surrounded by columns and covered walkways. Peristyle gardens in Pompeii, although highly decorative, were also found to produce food (Jashemski 1979, 32). Thus, a division between the ornamental and the practical garden was not necessarily observed.

Very little archaeological evidence for actual plant specimens survives (see Ciarallo 2000). Instead, we must rely on visual data provided by frescoes and wall paintings and on literary information provided by the ancient handbooks. Typical kitchen garden plants often mentioned in the sources include cabbage in all its varieties, asparagus, capers, parsley, mustard, and other herbs. Some plants were grown for medicinal purposes, others to provide nectar for bees. Romans also generally cultivated flowers that could be woven into garlands to adorn the family shrine and for festive occasions such as dinner parties.

Although concrete archaeological finds have much to teach us about the appearance and the function of the ancient Roman garden, it is important to bear in mind that what survives is most likely the evidence of élite life. Without the aid of electric pumps to circulate water, a continuous source of water in the form of a pool or fountain was available only to those who could afford to tap a water supply for such a superficial purpose. Often the pool in the middle of the peristyle garden was fenced off. Smaller gardens were enhanced by paintings of further gardens on back or side walls, affording an extended illusion of the garden. Seats and tables, and the characteristic *triclinium*, or three-sided dining couch, are also regularly found in gardens, attesting to their use as dining areas *al fresco*. Romans also adorned their gardens with sculptures of animals as well as deities. Many gardens are found to have small shrines at which a family could worship its tutelary deities. Thus, we can discern the variety of activities that took place in the Roman garden.

Above all, labour is the defining activity of the *hortus*. Cato, Varro, and Pliny the Elder all describe the painstaking work necessary to maintain a garden. In a candid fragment, the poet Gnaeus Matius (writing before Varro, who quotes Matius' Latin translations of Homer in his treatise on the Latin language) bluntly attests, 'I bestow more manure on my garden than I derive vegetables from it' (Courtney fr.

16). But with time – and with imperial wealth – gardens became sites of leisure as well, accompanied by a lexical shift from the singular *hortus* to the plural *horti* (see Boatwright 1998, 72n.7). Pliny the Elder credits Epicurus (the fourth/third century BCE Greek philosopher) as the first to use gardens for leisure:

> Nowadays indeed under the name of gardens (*hortorum nomine*) people possess the luxury of regular farms and country houses actually within the city. Epicurus, the master of ease, was the first to introduce the practice at Athens; up until his time it had not been the custom to have country dwellings in towns (*Natural History* 19.19).

For the wealthy who lived in the city of Rome, the garden became a place of private leisure, or *otium*, where one could regain the necessary strength to participate in the business, or *negotium*, of public life. A place of physical work became a symbolic retreat from political work. The most famous gardens of the late Republic (two of which figure prominently in this book) were established by men who overtly withdrew from politics but still remained in Rome: Lucullus, Maecenas, and Sallust (Wallace-Hadrill 1998, 2-6; Boatwright 1998, 72).

In a way that echoes Roman moralizing discourse, Lawson blames the shift in taste in Roman gardens, from simplicity to extravagance, on the prosperity that accompanied the growth of empire, when 'simple virtues were lost sight of and gave way before personal ambition and love of luxury' (1950, 105). In time, this disparity between the humble beginnings of the *hortus* and the luxurious capabilities of *horti* during the late Republic left Roman moral sensibilities in a deep predicament. Of course, one ought to seek the closeness to nature which the garden, an integral part of the humble Roman home, provides; on the other hand, it is easy to become indolent in the luxury of its peace and quiet. A *hortus* can be managed by one person; *horti*, on the other hand, require the labour of many. The difference between the *hortus* and the *horti* can also be measured in terms of fertility and sterility; the less useable produce a garden yields, the more morally suspect it becomes.

Originally set just beyond the *atrium* of the private house, between the dwelling and its uncultivated surroundings (e.g., Pliny *Natural*

History 19.60; Conan 1986, 349), the *hortus* occupied a space between nature and culture, where produce was harvested for its usefulness to society. Later, the grand *horti* of the Republic, designed more for aesthetic pleasure than for utility, were built on the edges of the city of Rome. Neither completely urban nor truly rural, the gardens of the late Republic that survived and flourished in the first century CE formed a ring around the crowded urban spaces of Rome (Kaster 1974, 15; Purcell 1987, 188). Thus both the simple *hortus* and the grand *horti* are characterized by peripheral locations.

This position in the landscape of both the kitchen garden and the luxury garden recapitulates the etymological origins of *hortus* meaning 'enclosure' (Ernout and Meillet 1959, 300 [s.v. *hortus*]; Grimal 1984, 41; van Erp-Houtepen 1986, 227). Investigating the etymology of the word 'garden' in Indo-European languages, van Erp-Houtepen concludes that 'the fence or wall is a basic and characteristic feature of the garden: a garden without a fence is in fact no longer a proper garden' (1986, 229). According to Carroll, the Persian word *pairidaeza* is derived from *pairi* meaning 'around,' and *daeza*, meaning 'wall' (2003, 124). Even the eighteenth-century gardens of the British Lancelot 'Capability' Brown, who designed gardens of unembellished topography, featured the 'ha-ha'. The edge of the garden was no longer a fence but a trench cut into the earth, indiscernible until stumbled upon, affording a laugh, a 'ha-ha' for the gardener (Mansbach 1982). Even in antiquity, the Romans sometimes saw fit to hide the garden enclosure; Pliny the Younger describes the elaborate stone wall around the garden at his Laurentian villa: 'The whole garden is enclosed by a dry-stone wall which is hidden from sight by a box hedge planted in tiers' (*Epistle* 5.6.17).

More often in Roman gardens, a boundary stone, a herm, or a statue of Janus marked the edge. Such boundaries were regarded as sacred, as Ovid attests when he describes the Terminalia, the festival of the god of boundaries: 'Terminus, whether you are a stone or a stump dug into the earth, you have always had divine status from of old' (*Fasti* 2.641-2). Boundaries and limits surround, define, and reassure by asserting ownership and imposing order in the face of chaos. The symbols of these boundaries bore religious significance for the Romans.

Often at the entrances to Renaissance gardens, a *lex horti* was inscribed on a stone, dictating the proper use of the garden. The *lex* ensured that one's conduct within the garden would be different from ordinary conduct in the 'secular' world (Morford 1987, 151-3). Like the artifice of the plants and fountains, the *lex* was a way of contriving the pleasure of the Renaissance garden. Thus, the control over nature that the garden exerts has its counterpart in the control of human nature (Pugh 1988, 102-3). Evidence from antiquity also attests to the posting of a *lex horti*. An inscription containing three rules for proper conduct was found on the wall overlooking the garden in the so-called House of the Moralist, excavated in Pompeii:

> The server shall wash and dry the guest's feet; a napkin shall protect the cushions and care shall be taken with the linen.
>
> Cast not lustful glances and make not eyes at another man's wife; be chaste in speech.
>
> Refrain from anger and insolent language, if you can; if not, return to your own house (*Corpus Inscriptionum Latinarum* 4.7698).

Two of these prescriptions are concerned with proper speech in the garden, but the final clause reiterates the principle of exclusion; any one exhibiting unwanted behaviour, like a weed, will be ejected from the garden.

Since gardens are characterized by the fence which denotes a definite boundary, they offer instances for transgression, and transgression is deeply rooted in the mythological foundation of Rome. While Romulus surrounded the Palatine Hill with a trench, his twin Remus criticized the paltry fortification. Angered by the criticism, Romulus ordered his men to take vengeance on anyone who crossed the trench. Remus jumped across and was killed. Wiseman calls this 'a too familiar story', in which it is easy to forget that the very walls of Rome were stained with the blood of fratricide (Wiseman 1995, 1). Like the foundation over which Remus leapt, boundaries define and are defined by violation. 'The limit and the transgression,' writes Foucault, 'depend on each other for whatever density of being they possess: a limit could not exist if it were absolutely uncrossable and, reciprocally, transgression would be pointless if it merely crossed a limit composed of illusions and shadows' (1977, 34).

In the landscape of ancient Rome, the late Republican gardens were located on the edges of the city, forming a boundary between *urbs* (city) and *rus* (country) not readily perceived. As they developed into luxurious pleasure retreats, the gardens of the wealthy came to symbolize extravagance. The etymology of 'extra-vagance' resonates if we consider the behaviour of the wealthy who, in 'wandering beyond' the forum, the place of duty and *negotium*, find ways to spend their *otium* and to display their wealth, the fruits of their ambition. How quickly a wide-eyed tour of a sunny, ancient Mediterranean garden can turn into a perilous voyage into the more polemical aspects of Roman politics and culture. We shall need a few landmarks by which to steer the course of our investigation.

III

The importance of the garden as a cultural artifact has been valorized by John Dixon Hunt, who offers new directions for the study of garden history. He calls for a more interdisciplinary approach to the field, recognizing the contribution that a history of gardens can make to a social history and a history of mentalité (Hunt 1999, 88). He also expands the possible sources for garden history beyond primary documents and material remains to include secondary sources. Literature about gardens, according to Hunt, 'can be a remarkable resource, if we are trying to understand how the phenomenal, material world of gardens is received in the minds and imaginations of those who encounter it' (Hunt 2004, 15). With this interdisciplinary approach that includes a wider range of sources, our understanding of the role of the garden in cultural history has advanced significantly. For instance, human societies invest gardens, very real palpable spaces, with intangible beliefs, myths, fictions, and illusions (Hunt 1997, 6). The nature of a garden always reflects the culture of the people who create it. Hunt suggests that rather than excavate the duality of nature and culture in the garden, instead we ought to recognize the power of the garden to meld nature and culture into what was recognized in the Renaissance as a *terza natura*, or a 'third nature' (Hunt 1991, 19; Beck 2002). In effect, the garden is an ongoing dialogue between nature and culture, a dialogue shaped by, but distinct from, its interlocutors.

Qualifications to this approach are necessary, otherwise the garden, with its hyper-elevated aesthetic status, loses its relevance to the world around it and becomes a mere fetish. Interpretation that disconnects the garden from the rest of society runs the risk of losing sight of the materialism of the garden. At the fore of material interpretation are concerns about the social relationships that the garden generates: Who owns it? Who tends it? Who may partake in its produce and pleasure? In response to Hunt's desideratum of the garden as a cultural object, Crozier (1999) insists that gardens are experienced both from within and without. The principle of exclusion that establishes the existence of the garden must account for the experience of that which is excluded as well.

In this sense, I find Helphand's discussion of defiant gardens at once exciting – and disappointing. Helphand brilliantly exposes the way gardens can demonstrate the human capacity for survival. Defiant gardens, which he defines as 'gardens created in extreme or difficult environmental, social, political, economic, or cultural conditions or situations' (1997, 103), champion the will to triumph and the indomitable persistence of the human spirit. He documents and illustrates defiant gardens in the trenches of World War I, the Warsaw ghetto, and the Japanese American internment camps, without sentimentalizing their redemptive powers. The history of gardens is no doubt the history of sanctioned gardens: Pompeii, Versailles, Stowe. But Helphand gives voice to these marginalized gardens and their expressions of existence and resistance.

Yet Helphand's analysis takes for granted that sanctioned gardens also make statements, every bit as strident and radical as defiant gardens; for sanctioned gardens create and perpetuate certain environmental, social, political, economic, or cultural conditions or situations. In this sense, all gardens defy. Some, as Helphand clearly shows, defy the status quo. Others, however, defy all that threatens the status quo. Thus, I submit that gardens are sites of contest: human against nature, to be sure, but more to the point, human against human. And I would amend Finlay's statement in the epigraph to this introduction, to say that *all* gardens are described as retreats, when really they are all attacks. All gardens exist on the principle of exclusion, all gardens shut out anything undesirable. We can be grateful for defiant gardens that seek to reclaim the human spirit,

13

effectively using the same medium as the oppressor. But we must also stay alert to the polemic of the garden, whatever its manifestation.

IV

Ancient Roman gardens are so captivating, and so difficult to study, because they are so distant from the modern experience, both temporally and spatially. Space and time determine how cultural information is encrypted in the garden. Such a simple statement, however, takes for granted a generally accepted definition of the words 'space' and 'time'. But these terms are far from stable or uncontested. Space may be commonly measured in geometrical terms (point, line, area, volume) and time recorded as the passage of discrete units (seconds, minutes, hours, days, weeks, months, years, decades, centuries, and millennia), but these terms of measurement are not universal. They agreed upon by any given society. The expressions of measurement can, and do, change according to social, cultural, and economic shifts in power; consider, for example, the primacy of the British over the metric system in the United States, or the use of a solar over a lunar calendar. Time and space are therefore anything but stable notions in their own right. Furthermore, Harvey (1990, 204) argues convincingly that 'neither time nor space can be assigned objective meanings independently of material processes'. If time and space are so integral to understanding the cultural meaning of the garden, then it is first necessary to acknowledge some of the ways that society can manipulate time and space.

Harvey (1990, 219-22) identifies four types of spatial regulators determined by society. First, the access to a given space and the cost of that accessibility is regulated by society. The accessibility to a given space determines the distance between individuals and the degree of hindrance or assistance to human interaction. The second regulator is appropriation: a space that is occupied by certain objects, activities, or individuals excludes the presence of other objects, activities, or individuals. Thirdly, domination refers to the degree of accessibility and appropriation that a person or group exerts over a given space. Finally, the production of space accounts for new systems of use, organization, and modes of representation. No doubt this is a highly cynical view of space, one that denies any validity to the commonplace notion that 'there is a time and a place for everything', that space is something to which all have equal access and equal opportunity. Although all beings occupy space, they do so according to social rules of accessibility, appropriation, dominance, and production. As we consider the space of the garden, it will be very useful to consider to whom that space is accessible, and how it is appropriated, dominated, and represented; such an approach will bring us closer to the social and cultural meaning of the garden.

The garden exhibits all of the characteristics of what Foucault (1986) calls 'heterotopias': constructed by society, a garden fulfils several functions, from food production to leisured aesthetics. Within its spaces, the garden contains a microcosm of the world, both natural (rock, wood, water, flora, fauna) and cultural (stakes, statuary, bridges, footpaths; see Thacker 1979, 29-31). Gardening is seasonal and thus a temporal activity. The area of a garden is separated from the rest of the landscape. A garden can be part of a larger agricultural network or part of a larger commercial organization. Gardens grow in relation to the rest of space, in relation to their surroundings; position in the garden is calculated according to cardinal points, water sources, sun, or shade. Thus, the term 'heterotopia' is a useful way to describe the spatial nature of the garden.

Time is no less difficult, no less polemical to define, and it is no less intimately connected with the society that experiences it. The progression of time from the past, things already experienced, to the present, to the future not yet experienced, seems natural. Yet society does not always fashion the experience of time in a linear form, from past to present to future. In a political revolution, the future takes precedence over all other time. Actions performed in the past are condemned for hindering the future, while actions performed in the present have value only if they contribute to the formation of the new state. In a patriarchal society, the past takes precedence over all other time. Nothing in the present compares to the value of the past, when things were better, stronger, and more effective. The best future is one that replicates the past. To express this antithesis in another way, progress is the opposite of a perception of time as decline; instead of getting worse, things only get better. Progress privileges the future, decline validates the past; both explain change teleologically. Cyclical time, on the other hand, accentuates not change but continuity and is a regular feature of religious, mythical, and magical societies. Whether an author chooses to represent time as teleological or cyclical (or both) proves significant in its implications for our understanding of the cultural meaning of the garden.

V

So far, I have described the garden as a place both physical and metaphysical, as a place of defiance and conformity, and as a place existing in space and time. Indeed, the degree of conformity or defiance is reflected by the use of space and time of the garden. Flourishing gardens planted in the trenches of World War I existed in a space and time that militated against the surrounding death and destruction. A garden located in Massachusetts may be modelled on a garden in Cornwall; a modern garden may replicate an ancient design. Conformity to the original denies the spatial or temporal distance between the two.

Before turning to my four gardens in Latin literature, it remains for me to establish my main avenue of approach to gardens in the Roman literary imagination. Because interpretations of gardens tend to range widely, Elkins (1993) argues that gardens are difficult to write about objectively. He identifies two poles that demarcate the continuum of interpretive analysis. At one end are the objective studies of the concrete elements of a particular garden; at the other end are the subjective essays on the abstract meanings of a garden. As if in opposition to one another, these two approaches never seem to recognize the contributions, or even the existence, of the other.

Elkins attempts to explain this disjunction in the conceptual analysis of gardens. Gardens, he says, are 'like mild soporifics' (1993, 196), producing a state close to hypnosis and dream. Because gardens break down the conceptual boundary between the conscious and the unconscious, writing about gardens is likewise rhetorically fragmented. He cites as an example the contributions in the edited volume of essays, *The Meaning of Gardens* (Francis and Hester 1990). The editors' introduction on the garden as 'idea, place, and action', exhibits some of the rhetoric that typifies the genre, in particular the repeated use of lists in place of formal argument. Antithesis contributes to the sense of disjointed prose. For example:

16

Introduction

In the garden as in society, there is an ongoing battle of seeming oppositions: male versus female, good versus evil, reaction versus revolution, self versus community, consumerism versus self-reliance, connectedness versus anomie, integration versus segregation, rich versus poor, real versus surreal, bigness versus smallness, sacred versus profane, science versus intuition, high versus folk art (Francis and Hester 1990, 4).

In addition to such sets of oppositions, gardens are frequently conceived of as representations; some gardens are constructed to resemble paintings, while some paintings clearly represent specific gardens. The garden is also employed as a central image of life's course from birth to death. In this sense the garden is so deeply rooted in the human psyche as to go beyond representation and to elicit desire, 'a kind of longing that operates without a specific object in mind and without relation to other people' (Elkins 1993, 191).

In short, Elkins equips us with three approaches to garden writing. Gardens are envisioned as sets of polarities or oppositions, as narratives of human life, and as open-ended sites of desire. He argues that these characteristics demonstrate that gardens induce a certain quality of thought. On the trail of the garden in the Roman literary imagination, then, these are the footsteps to follow: descriptions of gardens in terms of antithesis and polarity, as metaphors for life, and as a stimulus of unfulfilled desires and longings. Does the author allow himself to be so carried away by the pleasures of the garden as to abandon rational analysis? The presence of the author in garden writing and his assertions of self and responsibility help gauge the garden's transformative effect on the literary imagination. Eventually the garden becomes the setting for one of the most dramatic psychological transformations in classical literature, the religious conversion of Augustine to Christianity; however, the obvious place to begin an investigation of gardens in Roman literature is with the garden poem of the Neronian Columella.

17

1

The Garden of Empire

The dull necessity of weeding arises, because every
healthy plant is a racist and an imperialist; every
daisy (even) wishes to establish for itself an Empire on
which the sun never sets.

Ian Hamilton Finlay

On Agriculture is a twelve-book treatise by Junius Moderatus Columella from Gades (modern Cadiz), a town in the province of Baetica
in Southern Spain. The little we know about him is gleaned from his
surviving work, but we can surmise that he was a contemporary of
Seneca the Younger (4 BCE – 65 CE) and that he finished his treatise
in the later years of his life, during the reign of the emperor Nero. An
inscription records that he served in the Roman army as an officer of
the sixth legion, which was stationed for a time in Syria (*Inscriptiones
Latinae Selectae* 2923). The inscription was found at Tarentum in
southern Italy, where perhaps Columella died and was buried (Forster
1950 gives a concise account of the life of Columella).

Each of the twelve books of *On Agriculture* covers a particular
aspect of the farm: situation and quality of soil, water, farm buildings
and farmhands; fertilization of soil; care of vines; and the care of
livestock, dogs, birds, fish, and bees. After nine books of didactic prose,
however, in Book 10 Columella launches into 436 hexameters on the
cultivation of gardens (*cultus hortorum*), in a poem intended to sup-
plement the *Georgics* of Vergil. Books 11 and 12 revert to prose form,
treating, in turn, the duties of the *villicus* or overseer, and lastly the
overseer's wife and her management of the household. Book 10 feels
like a finale; Books 11 and 12, like afterthoughts (see Milnor 2005, 258
for perceptive remarks, also Henderson 2002). The exceptionality of
the garden – and the exceptionality of hexameter poetry in the midst
of prose – makes Columella's *On Agriculture* 10 an excellent starting
point for our investigation of literary representations of gardens. I

shall set aside for the moment the complicated relationship between *On Agriculture* 10 and Vergil's *Georgics* and begin with the physical and metaphysical features of Columella's garden poem, its treatment of time and space, and finally the evidence of the author's awareness of the garden's effect on his subconscious.

II

The poem begins with a proem naming the dedicatee (1-5), immediately followed by verses describing the suitable terrain for a garden (6-34) and an invocation to the Muses, traditional in didactic poetry (35-40). The design of the poem follows the course of a solar year, beginning with the autumnal equinox (41-54); in winter, the farmer prepares the soil (55-76). Most of the poem is devoted to the activities of the spring (77-310) and the produce of the summer (311-422). After a brief return to autumn (423-32) the poem closes with a four-line *envoi* (433-6) that harks back to Vergil.

Both flowers and produce grow in Columella's garden and the poem is rich with imagery that stimulates all five senses. Red elderberries, white lilies, blue hyacinths, purple violets, gold and purple pansies, and red roses, to name but a few flowers, awaken the sense of sight throughout the poem. The gardener is advised to choose a quiet plot of land undisturbed by the constant croaking of frogs (11-12). The reader is reminded, however, of the less pleasant smells in a garden by the image of fertilizer obtained from 'whatever the toilet pours forth from its filthy sewer pipes' (85). In terms of taste, the artichoke goes well with wine (235-6), and water is especially sweet to drink when it is just the right temperature, neither too warm nor too cold (284-5). The cool shadow of the late summer (379) contrasts with the heat against which the gardener must protect his plants (320-1). Columella's garden poem engages all five senses.

Once a proper site is determined for the garden, it should be enclosed by 'walls or rough hedges, so as to keep out cattle and thieves' (27-8). The first step is always to construct a definite border to keep unwanted things out, rather than hold necessary things in. The description of furrows for seeds is evocative: 'But now when the shining earth, combed with clear division marked, its filth abandoned, demands her seeds ...' (94-5). Within the boundaries of the garden, order

20

is created out of chaos, and clear distinctions are imposed upon the earth since any untidiness or filth must be cast out. In the most physical of terms, then, the garden is maintained by the meticulous upkeep of boundaries. The tangible distinctions of the garden, walls that exclude, furrows that are straight and narrow, and weeds that must be eliminated, are strong images that easily become metaphors for society.

Hard labour is required to create and maintain the garden, and the poet gives his orders to the workers. Tilling is a particularly forceful and violent activity. The earth is stripped of her clothes, her back lashed like a slave's. (Perhaps the slaves who rend the earth transfer – and thereby cope with – the violence inflicted upon their own flesh?) Finally, the earth is disembowelled:

> But look! A ceaseless and more back-breaking labour beckons: come, now drive away lazy sleep, and tear to pieces her green hair with ploughshare of curved tooth, now rend the weeds that clothe her. You, with heavy rakes dig through her resisting back; you, do not hesitate to uproot from the depths her bowels with broad hooks (67-73).

Providing water is also a labour-intensive task, rivalled only by the work of weeding:

> First I warn you to bring in large sources of water, so that thirst may not burn the seed shooting forth a bud. But when the fertile earth throws off her bonds and flowery offspring sprouts forth from mother soil, then let the gardener carefully watering pro-vide moderate showers for the first fruits of the plant and comb the ground with two-pronged fork and cast strangling weeds from the furrows (143-9).

Even more work is required if the garden does not have ready access to a water source; the gardener is advised to elevate the beds on mounds of dirt he must construct (150-3).

In addition to the physicality of the garden, Columella also creates a poem richly imbued with abstract imagery. For example, the poet alludes to several different Greek and Roman myths. He refers to the

21

constellation Corona Borealis as 'Bacchus' Cnossian passion' (52), a reference to Ariadne, daughter of Minos king of Cnossos; when she married Bacchus she was given a crown (*corona*) that was placed in the sky. The exhortation to the farmer to rend the earth violently (67-73) is justified by recalling the myth of Deucalion, for the earth is no stranger to violence. When the earth was consumed in a fierce flood and humankind was almost utterly destroyed, Deucalion and Pyrrha regenerated the human race by tearing rocks from the tall mountains and casting them over their shoulders (60-7). The wanton revelry of Venus and Cupid is an allegory for the onset of spring (197-9). The rain in springtime is as gentle as the shower of gold that Jupiter rained on Danae (204-6).

Such mythological allusions link the individual garden to the rest of the universe and demonstrate its importance in the cosmic order. They were no doubt conventional features of poetry for post-Hellenistic poets striving to demonstrate their learning and expertise. In addition to mythological allusions, Columella also seasons the poem with clever plays on Greek words. He versifies the names of famous Greek sculptors (Polyclitus, Phradmon, and Ageladas, 30). He wittily mentions the herb *lepidium*, or pepperwort:

(Now is the time to sow) ... the herb that tempers the taste of milk, used to remove the brands from the foreheads of runaways, thereby declaring its own usefulness in a Greek name (124-6).

Although Columella does not name *lepidium*, by referring to the herb's ability to remove tattoos, he suggests its etymology from the Greek verb *lepizein*, to peel off skin. Again, similarly in a clever riddle, Columella plays on the double meaning of the word *beta*, both as a vegetable and as the second letter of the Greek alphabet. Summer is the time to sow the 'beta', beet:

And next the plant of Greek name, just as the letter next to the first is imprinted in the wax by the stylus of the learned teacher, so too is it implanted in the fertile soil with the stroke of the iron-shod spade, the *beta* (beet), green in leaf, white in root (251-4).

1. The Garden of Empire

Thus by naming famous artists, and by referring to pepperwort and beets, Columella is able to demonstrate his knowledge of Greek culture and language and give his Latin poem a cosmopolitan flavour. As Gowers demonstrates, this poem is much more 'pretentious' than Columella would lead the reader to believe (Gowers 2000, 140). In effect, Columella demonstrates that gardens are a suitable subject for hexameter poetry that can accommodate all the expectations of the genre.

Perhaps the most pervasive feature of the poem is religion. The roses harvested from the garden fill the temples of the gods with their sweet fragrance (260-2). When invoking Proserpina to return from the Underworld and bring fertility with her, Columella promises there will be no tricks or snares: 'We worship pure Faith and sacred household gods' (278-9). And from the very beginning, once the walls of the garden are established, the gardener must erect a wooden statue of Priapus for protection:

> Worship the divinity Priapus terrifyingly ithyphallic, hewn from the trunk of an old tree, who always in the middle of the garden threatens the boy with his swollen groin and the thief with his sickle (31-4).

Believed to be the son of Aphrodite and Dionysus, this rustic divinity is generally held to have originated in Lampsacus. The ithyphallic god was associated with sexuality and by extension fertility. It seems that the scarecrow-like Priapus was stationed in the garden for two reasons. His oversized red penis, his chief characteristic and his only attribute, was an apotropaic symbol that warded off the evil eye and thereby granted fertility, while the threatening size of his member was also meant to ward off thieves.

The *Priapea*, a first-century CE collection of eighty Latin poems about Priapus, contains several epigrams about the violent and obscene punishment thieves will experience if Priapus catches them in his garden. For example:

> Whoever lifts thieving hands against this little plot of land entrusted to me will know that I am not a eunuch (Parker 15.1-3).

23

I warn you, you can't deny it. If you come here as a thief, you will leave as a catamite (Parker 59).

When desire for the fig overcomes you and you wish to reach a hand this way, look upon me, thief, and think about what a heavy cock you will have to shit back out (Parker 69).

In these poems, the punishment, whether implied or explicit, is always the same: Priapus will anally rape anyone who violates the plot of land he guards. To the Roman way of thinking, boundaries were so important that they demanded the protection of gods both sacred and profane. Terminus, god of boundary stones, was venerated in a solemn festival on a specified day. On the other hand, Priapus was expected to protect the garden every day by the most violent and humiliating means imaginable.

When spring brings a rich harvest of flowers, Columella's gardener is told to fill his basket with roses and marigolds,

so that rich in spring's merchandise Vertumnus may abound, and with staggering gait, soaked with much wine, the porter may bring back from the city pockets full of money (308-10).

Vertumnus was an Etruscan god of the harvest, celebrated in a poem by Propertius (4.2) that describes his ability to assume various appearances – hence his name, derived in folk etymology from the Latin *vertere*, to change. A statue of Vertumnus stood in Rome on the Vicus Tuscus, a street that entered the Sacra Via between the Temple of Castor and the Basilica Julia, connecting the Forum Romanum with the Forum Boarium, the cattle market on the bank of the Tiber. There was also a temple to Vertumnus on the Aventine hill (Radke 1965, 317-20). Vertumnus, in his capacity for change, is also associated with the god Janus, whose temple also stood between the Forum Romanum and the Forum Boarium. The two-faced Janus, looking forward and backward simultaneously, was a potent symbol of commerce, trade, and thereby profit; his bifrontal image appears regularly on Republican coinage. Thus the mention of Vertumnus calls forth images of Rome's business district and its other patron deity, Janus. Yet something in this porter's profitable return chafes uncomfortably against a portrait of otherwise rustic simplicity. If everyone engaged in proper gardening, there would be no need for markets, no demand for the gardener to supply. Self-sufficiency, however, seems to be an ideal, reserved for some and not others.

Furthermore, Ovid relates a legend that Vertumnus fell in love with Pomona, a nymph quite skilled in horticulture (*Metamorphoses* 14.623-771). So dedicated was she to her gardening that she vowed to avoid men and remain a virgin. After disguising himself as a reaper, a leaf-gatherer, a vine-pruner, a soldier, and a fisherman, Vertumnus finally turned himself into an old woman who successfully persuaded Pomona to take a husband. Ovid weaves a tale of boundary transgression; the binary opposition of male/female, blurred by Vertumnus' transvestism, is mapped onto the garden's topography. The female interior of Pomona's garden is penetrated by Vertumnus; however, the result is not the annihilation of the garden, but its ultimate fertility. No doubt the virgin Pomona, tending her plants, had dirt under her nails. So Columella's very brief mention of Vertumnus in his garden poem mobilizes the simultaneously twin-textured lore of this urban commercial and rustic Italian god and reminds the reader that whatever the garden may transcend, it still has its roots in the soil, it still depends on labour.

At this point in the poem, Columella lists some of the possible pests and blights of the garden: snails, caterpillars, hail, and heavy dew that spawns worms. Indeed, a comprehensive garden poem includes all the things the gardener needs to exclude from the real garden (Gowers 2000, 140). The gardener should take care to appease the deity Robigus, who averts mildew from the plants, with the sacrifice of a puppy (342-3). Columella describes how destruction was warded off in legendary times:

Hence Etruscan Tages is said to have set up at the edge of his fields the head of an Arcadian ass-colt, stripped of its skin; and often did Tarchon encircle his abodes with the white vines to ward off the thunderbolts of mighty Jove. Hence the son of Amythaon, learning much from Chiron, suspended the birds of night from forked sticks and forbade them to wail their doleful notes from the high housetops (344-50).

Tages was a descendant of Jupiter who was supposed to have invented the Etruscan art of haruspicy (divination by means of inspecting an animal's liver). During the Republic, it was standardized through practice until it gained permanent status in Roman state religion. Hence Tages' method would have been considered venerable, if not reliable. The hero Tarchon was the eponymous founder of the Etruscan city of Tarquinia who commanded the forces of Aeneas, founder of Rome. Thus, he lends the poem a sense of pride in Roman identity and statehood. The son of Amythaon was a famous doctor, and Chiron the centaur was a teacher of heroes.

After the bizarre rituals from legendary times, Columella then dispenses rather more practical advice:

> To keep baneful creatures from plucking the tender crops, it has been found useful at times to steep the seeds and sprinkle them with the oily and unsalted lees of the olive or to saturate them with the natural black soot of the hearth. It has also been useful to pour upon the plants the bitter juices of horehound, and to moisten them unsparingly with the sap of the houseleek (351-6).

Religion appears to give way to pragmatism; however, even these remedies can fail and the final suggestion to ward off the most desperate plague from the garden is not scientific but deeply superstitious:

> But if no drug can banish the plague, then let the arts of the magician Dardanus be used, and a barefoot woman, observing for the first time the regular laws of womanhood, shamed by the flow of her disgusting blood, but with garments loosened and hair unbound, is led three times around the beds and hedges of the garden (357-62).

Thus, though the garden is the product of hard labour, it is also a place imbued with superstitious ritual. The physicality of the garden calls forth mythological, intellectual, and religious associations. The physical commingles with the metaphysical.

III

Columella's treatment of time and space in his poem also reveals much about the garden in the literary imagination and its capability to express certain cultural codes. The most striking example is the statement that 'as many as are the varieties, so many are the times for sowing every kind' (189). Caecilian lettuce is planted in January, Cappadocian in February; his own Spanish lettuce is planted in March, and Cyprian sown in April (190-3). For every variety from every corner of the world, there is a proper time; however, the notion that there is 'a time and a place for everything' elides the fact that not everyone has access to time and space equally. Such a formulation of proper times for proper things implies that time and space can be assigned objective meanings independently of material processes. Representations of time and space reveal the underlying ideologies of Columella's garden poem.

Time and its passing are specified in a variety of ways throughout the poem. Four months of the year are not mentioned by name but are alluded to indirectly (190-3). The constellation 'Aquarius' refers to January; this astrological allusion calls to mind the practices of celestial divination and the lore that accompanied each constellation. Although astrology had practical applications (it was useful to determine the changes of seasons, to measure time, to navigate through land or sea), it was also used to conjecture about the future. Thus, the reference to January as 'Aquarius' suggests the importance of the farmer's ability to read the stars and divine the future. The next three months, February, March, and April, are called 'Lupercus' (whose festival occurs in February), 'Mars' (the god of March), and 'the Paphian' (i.e., Venus, to whom April was sacred). Time is thus given religious significance as well.

Eight dates are specified in the poem, designated by the rising of certain constellations. According to Marshall (1918, 121-2):

When the Dog Star drinks deep the Ocean's waves (41) = September 24
And Titan balances the world between equal hours (42) = September 26, i.e., the autumnal equinox

Atlas' daughters fear the rising sun's opposing rays (54) =
October 28
Phoebus, fearful, flees the claws and stings of Scorpio (56) =
November 18
Orpheus' lyre deserts the starry pole (79) = February 3
When the prince of stars and flocks lifts his head above the waves
(156) = March 23
When Titan extends the day with his twin flames (312) = May 19
When Sirius, Dog of Erigone, kindled by Hyperion's heat opens
fruit upon the trees (400-1) = August 20

Thus time is measured by the position, the spatial relation, of stars in
the sky; this conception of time in terms of space underscores the
physicality of the garden. Clearly time is important to the gardener;
he must be attuned to the changing of the seasons and the different
activities each season demands for the cultivation of the garden.
Furthermore, Columella need outline only one year's calendar, since
the entire cycle repeats itself. But the dates are given in astrological
terms; the gardener must be in tune with the stars. Time can pass
unnoticed, with silent step and no sound (159-60); therefore the gardener must be vigilant, for the skies provide the only predictable
indication of time's passing. The calendar is written in the sky, revealing only the present constellations. The gardener must anticipate the
rising and setting of constellations but views only the present configu-
ration of stars. Thus, while time appears to be an eternal and connected cycle, the constellations designate time in discrete units. All
of these aspects of time in the garden poem are expanded upon in
Book 11, in a calendar of works and days (much like the *Works and
Days*, a Greek wisdom poem of the archaic poet Hesiod) that describes time in mythological, religious, and astronomical terms and
reinforces with every entry in the calendar that there is a time for
everything.

The encyclopaedic quality of Columella's poem, with its catalogues
of unfamiliar plants, is a regular feature of Roman agricultural literature, found in the works of Cato and Varro before him, and Pliny the
Elder after him. Although tedious to modern aesthetic sensibilities
and often incomprehensible because of their obscure allusions, the
catalogues nevertheless can reveal insights about an author's assump-

tions or methods of composition. Columella's list of places where cabbage grows exposes his particular perception of space:

> Many places produce cabbage, including ancient Cumae on turf-clad shore, the Marrucine lands, Signia on the Lepine mountain's side, Capua's rich plains, garden plots near the Caudine Forks, Stabiae known for its fountains, Vesuvian fields, learned Parthenope near the dewy stream of Sebethis, the sweet Pompeian marsh near the Herculean salt-pits where Siler rolls his crystal waters down. The hardy Sabine land also produces a stem with many shoots, as does the land near Turnus' lake, in fields of Tibur where the fruit trees grow, and the Bruttian lands, and Aricia, home of the leeks (130-9).

Columella says that the cabbage grows throughout the whole world (*toto ... terrae / orbe*, 127-8), but the specific places mentioned are all located on the Italian peninsula, mostly south of Rome. Beginning at Cumae in Campania, Columella then mentions the Marrucine lands, which are due north and directly across the peninsula; Signia lies forty miles south east of Rome, Capua and the Caudine Forks in the heart of Campania. Stabiae, Mount Vesuvius, learned Parthenope (Naples), and Herculaneum are all on the Bay of Naples. Turnus' lake is in Latium; Tibur is the modern Tivoli, only fifteen miles east of Rome; the Bruttian lands cover the 'toe' of Italy, and Aricia is south east of Rome. By sowing such a simple, unassuming vegetable as the cabbage, the gardener can bring into his plot a plant that grows in many different regions of southern Italy. This common plant, profusely praised by Cato for its medicinal purposes (*On Agriculture* 156-7), unites the individual garden plot with other Italian gardens.

Herbs from beyond Italy, however, are also found in Columella's garden:

> Now let crocus plants scented thanks to foreign lands descend from the Sicilian mountains of Hybla and now let marjoram born from gay Canopus come, and let there be Achaian myrrh that imitates your tears, virgin daughter of Cinyras, yet richer in myrrh-oil (169-73).

Aphrodisiacs from Megara and Africa (106-7) and parsnips from Syria (114) likewise grow in Columella's garden. He describes the various shapes of gourds and their uses; especially round gourds make good containers for pitch from the Greek colony Naryx in Bruttium in southern Italy or for honey from Mount Hymettus in Attica (386). Lettuce too comes from exotic places. Two varieties, presumably from Africa, are named after Caecilius Metellus, a consul in the First Punic War.

> The third, which is pale with thick but smooth tip, preserves in its own name that of the Cappadocian people. And my own variety, which Gades produces on the shore of Tartessus, is white with curled foliage and white stem. Likewise the variety which Cyprus cultivates in rich, Paphian soil, has reddish leaf but milky stalk (183-8).

At the end of the poem, autumn harvest provides one final opportunity to display fruits from around the world in the garden: plums from Armenia and Damascus; peaches from Persia, Gaul, and Asia; figs from Caria, Chios, the Chelidonian islands, Libya, and Lydia; and turnips from Nursia, a small Sabine town (404-22).

Columella's garden contains specimens from across the ancient Mediterranean and is thereby a small parcel that represents a terrestrial totality. When spring arrives at his garden, it compels 'the seas, the mountains, and in short, the entire world' to rejoice (209-10). His garden is capable of juxtaposing several distant, foreign lands within one unique place. Spain, Gaul, Africa, Asia, Greece and its islands – all regions under Roman rule – are condensed into one space and meet in the singular, single garden. Like the garden that is capable of producing fruit from many foreign lands in one well-ordered microcosm, so the Roman empire brings foreign lands and peoples under one vast, well-ordered administration. Empire is naturalized; it is as ordinary a phenomenon as a tender herb garden or a finely pruned orchard.

IV

I have tried to show that Columella's seemingly innocent and rather monotonous poem about the cultivation of the garden reveals a sophisticated conception of the physical and metaphysical possibilities of the garden and the ideological uses of time and space in the garden. But how aware was Columella of his particular interpretations of the garden? The obvious place to look is the prose preface that precedes the poem.

Columella dedicates *On Agriculture* to an otherwise unknown, but intriguingly named Publius Silvinus; Henderson calls him 'Woody' (2004, 51). Thus, the name of the dedicatee of *On Agriculture* evokes images of clearing the ground for cultivation, ridding the ground of 'woods' whose timber can be used as raw material. Columella evidently sent Silvinus individual books upon completion (since Columella responds to his comments in subsequent books). Although each book begins with an address to Silvinus, only Books 9, 10, and 12 begin with formal prefaces. Columella felt it necessary to introduce the rather diverse material of Book 9 with a preface that serves as a sort of table of contents. The preface to Book 12, on the other hand, justifies the topics included because they had been treated by Xenophon in his *Oeconomicus*, a work which Cicero saw fit to translate into Latin. But the preface to Book 10 serves yet another purpose.

Columella begins by asking Silvinus to receive Book 10 as the last remaining payment of his balance due; the previous nine books paid the debt except for this final instalment: 'Here is the garden poem, payment in full' (*Pref.* 1). Next he announces the topic of the book: *cultus hortorum*, the cultivation of gardens (*Pref.* 1). The subject has a particular immediacy, claims Columella, because nowadays with the increase in luxurious dining and the rise in food prices, common people are reduced to consuming ordinary fare (*Pref.* 2). In further defence of his subject matter, Columella notes that the treatises of Cato and Varro are not comprehensive, while Vergil passed up the topic of gardens altogether in the *Georgics*. Then he continues:

> This book, as I had decided, would be joined to the earlier books in prose, were it not for your constant demand that wore down my intention, instructing me to finish in poetic measures the missing parts of the *Georgics*, which even Vergil himself expressly stated that he left to later generations to relate (*Pref.* 3).

At work in this statement is the convention of the literary request, explored by White in Cicero and the Augustan poets (1993, 64-78).

Although the language that a writer employs to describe the literary demand appears at first strikingly urgent and forceful, such language is testimony only to the recipient's perception of the demand. It is not an accurate indicator of the intensity of the request. Columella's statement, 'your constant demand', is a good example of this herme-neutic. However much Silvinus may have pestered Columella for the completion of Book 10, surely Columella had already organized the material into ten, if not twelve, distinct units whose completion was demanded as much by the formal structure of *On Agriculture* as it was by its dedicatee. What Silvinus seems to have influenced was the choice of medium: only because of his persistent requests did Co-lumella relent and compose Book 10 in verse.

The rest of the preface openly expresses an uneasiness with the poem's status vis-à-vis the *Georgics* (on references to Vergil through-out Columella's treatise, see Cossarini 1977; Noè 2002, 163). Columella states that he undertook the challenge of writing in verse, further compelled by the divine majesty (*numine instigante*) of Vergil himself, only out of a desire to venerate the poet most highly. Then, the grammar of the preface takes an almost imperceptible turn. First person singular verbs shift to the first person plural. Of course, it is common for Latin authors to use the first person plural to refer to themselves alone, as indeed Columella does several times in his poem (lines 60, 140-3, 279, 425, 430). But in the preface, I believe the first person plural takes on a special significance:

> We have attempted a subject quite minor and practically devoid of substance, a subject so insignificant that in the completion of our entire corpus, it can be counted as just one small part of our overall output (*Pref.* 4).

Such prefatory rhetoric of modesty is one means by which an author attempts to secure the reader's goodwill. He lowers the reader's expec-tations so that he or she will be pleasantly surprised at how deftly the author handles the material. He also deflects blame for the shortcom-ings of his work on to the subject matter itself and away from his skill as a poet. What if Columella's use of the first person plural also indirectly implicates Vergil in this self-effacing pose? 'We have burned the midnight oil' (*elucubravimus*), says Columella, perhaps implying

32

that he has worked as hard as Vergil on his poem. By agreeing to take up the subject of *cultus hortorum* at all, Columella outstrips Vergil, who did not give over space – or time – to write verses on such a difficult subject matter. 'But now let us put an end to the foreword' (*Pref.* 5). Again the plural suggests that both authors must proceed, Columella taking up Vergil's voice, completing the poems of both. Columella both reveres and identifies with his predecessor.

The overall effect of the preface levels the competition. Vergil may be the champion, but Columella is a formidable contender because he is willing to pick up where Vergil left off (and it is worth remembering that Vergil himself followed in the path of Varro; see Leach 1984 and Thomas 1987). The compliment to Vergil is tempered; neither is it the hollow insincerity or abject adulation often perceived in Neronian literature, nor is it solely an admission of poetic inferiority. Like Ovid before him and Statius after him, Columella as successor of Vergil passes judgement on the very poet he holds up as exemplary. It is interesting to note that Ovid and Statius reserve their judgements of Vergil for the last books of their epic poems, *Metamorphoses* 15 and *Thebaid* 12. In contrast, Columella adds two more books of *On Agriculture* after his nod to Vergil. Finally, it is worth noting that Columella is not the only Neronian writer to interrupt prose with hexameter verse in a move at once laudatory and critical. In a fragment of Petronius' *Satyricon*, Eumolpus recites a 295-line epyllion that engages with the epic *Bellum Civile* by Lucan, one of the leading court poets of Neronian Rome. As Columella interrupts his prose to emulate his forerunner Vergil, so Petronius interrupts his prose to emulate his coeval Lucan. Both Columella and Petronius introduce their metrical interruptions with distinct statements of literary criticism. Both authors enter the poetic melee only to retreat to the shelter of prose.

The poem is framed by the poet's first person voice. Columella's hexameters begin:

Silvinus, I will also teach you horticulture and the things that Vergil once left to those of us after him to recount, prevented as he was by limited space in his poem of fertile fields, the gifts of Bacchus, you Great Pales, and heavenly honey (1-5).

This opening is easily recognized as an imitation of *Georgics* 4.147-8, 'But these topics I myself, prevented by limited space, leave for others to recount after me.' In these lines, Vergil closes a digression in *Georgics* 4 that begins with an over-determined nine-line apology for having included the passage. If I were not so close to the end of the work, says Vergil, I would sing of the garden, its roses, endive, parsley, gourd, narcissus, acanthus, ivy, and myrtle (4.116-24). The next twenty-two lines describe an old Corycian gardener, whom Vergil imagines dwelling in the refuge of the garden and reaping its produce. For Johnson, the 'core of this passage' seeks an alternative to the political, social, and even economic realities. The digression, separated so markedly from the rest of the narrative, vividly demonstrates the separateness of the garden. The problem, of course, is that such a retreat to a place of complete separation can be achieved only in the imagination (Johnson 2004, 82).

We can only guess why Vergil stopped himself from writing about a garden. The constraints of space are a poor and unconvincing excuse. Perhaps he was unwilling to lend himself to such a powerfully trans-formative topic. Perhaps he found the garden to be a frustratingly unsatisfying topic. Perhaps he was exercising that characteristically Vergilian ability to keep the obvious and dangerously banal at arm's length. Whatever the reason, the result is the same: because Vergil did not versify a garden, anyone who did is judged inferior for not heeding the wise silence of Rome's premier poet. Damned if you dare to meet him head on, damned if you steer clear of him, Vergil stymied Latin poetry even as he distilled it.

Columella's final hexameters conclude with an explicit reference to Vergil, who is, quite literally, first (*primus*) and last:

> So far, Silvinus, I have been teaching you about horticulture, relating the precepts of the divine poet Vergil, who first (*primus*) daring to reveal the ancient sources sang the Hesiodic song throughout Roman villages (433-6).

This is likewise, and suitably, a quotation from *Georgics* 2.175-6, 'daring to reveal the ancient sources, I sing the Hesiodic song through-out Roman villages.' These are the clearest moments of the presence of the author in the garden poem and of his assertions of self and responsibility. These statements point to the author's anxiety of influence. But can we detect in the poem an anxiety of inspiration, that is, an awareness of the transformative effect of the subject matter on the poet's psyche?

Halfway through the poem, Columella stops himself with a revealing question:

> But why am I, carried off along a lofty path, boldly allowing my horses to fly through the air in unbridled course? Those wonders are sung by him whom the Delphic laurel urged on to the causes of things (215-18).

He has just described the coming of spring in elegant terms that recall the descriptions of fertility and growth in Vergil. Columella realizes that he has got carried away, and that his excitement over the subject-matter has caused him to stray from his strictly didactic mode. He wakes from this temporary reverie:

> Calliope now recalls me from my wanderings and orders me to run the narrow course and with her compose in simple style verses which to the accompaniment of the Muse the pruner may sing while working among the branches, the gardener among his green gardens (225-9).

He reminds himself of his audience, and he writes not merely for his own enjoyment, but for the edification of the gardener. His treatise, though aesthetically pleasing, must first fulfil its educational goal. This is the point at which Columella reels in his inclination to allow the garden to run away with his senses (Henderson 2004, 15-16). This, I believe, is good evidence of what Elkins calls the 'mild soporific', the ability of the garden to induce a certain frame of mind (1993, 196). Something about gardens transforms those who write about them, inducing a trance-like mode that abandons rational analysis and revels in the beauty and pleasure of the moment (see also Pugh 1988, 106). Columella is not exempt from such a transformation. After more than two hundred verses on the best type of soil, the best situation for the garden, the best time to plant, he is overwhelmed by the remarkable beauty of his subject matter. By deliberately recalling himself to

35

the task at hand, Columella admits his momentary lapse and exposes the seductive power of the garden.

In the *Georgics*, Vergil comes to the garden by way of bees: 'Let there be gardens fragrant with saffron flowers to invite [the bees], and let the watchman against thieves and birds, guardian Priapus, lord of the Hellespont, protect them with his willow-hook' (*Georgics* 4.109-11). If he were not nearing the end of his poem, 'perhaps, too, I might be singing what careful tillage decks rich gardens' (*forsitan ... canerem, Georgics* 4.118-19). Indeed, the contrary to fact condition renders this digression on the Corycian farmer a sort of *recusatio*, if you will, a polite refusal to engage in a particular poetic subject (see Lyne 1995, 31-9). Vergil proceeds for some twenty-five more lines before recalling himself: 'But these topics I myself, prevented by limited space, leave for others to recount after me' (*Georgics* 4.147-8). Vergil, momentarily exposed to the transformative powers of the garden, awakens from his reverie so as *not* to finish the work of writing about the garden. Perhaps of all the ways that Columella's Book 10 supplements Vergil's *Georgics*, Columella's expression of the disparity in the conceptual analysis of gardens most fully brings the *Georgics* to completion. Columella awakens from his reverie for the sole purpose of finishing his – and Vergil's – garden narrative.

As we proceed to readings of Horace's *Satire* 1.8, Tacitus' *Annals* 11, Augustine's *Confessions* 8, and Stoppard's *Arcadia*, we shall be looking for just such transformative moments of admission and exposition. As even the most ornate garden strives to give the impression of simplicity, purity, and even divinity, so it also obscures the underlying principle of exclusion, allowing some living things to thrive within its borders at the expense of others. A garden is a site of pleasure only for those granted privileged access. The gardener's job is to weed out anything and anyone undesirable. The maintenance of boundaries often involves force, and the maintenance of the garden is no exception. It is a site of perpetual contest. In the next chapter, we shall explore a satirical poem of Horace in which the scarecrow Priapus polices the boundary of a garden – transformed from a cemetery – and drives out one of the most transgressive types of women in western culture: a witch.

2

The Garden of Politics

A garden is not an object but a process.

Ian Hamilton Finlay

I

'Satire is totally ours,' says Quintilian, the first-century CE teacher of rhetoric and author of the *Institutes of Oratory*. He cannot mean that Romans invented the notion of sexually and scatologically aggressive invective, bombast, or irony; plenty of Greek poetry remains to testify to its prevalence long before the satirists of Rome seized upon such material. Rather, the statement more likely indicates that these elements were mixed together into satire and so transformed by Roman writers into a successful medium for expressing ideas distinctively Roman. For Freudenburg (2001), the constant carping about the degeneracy of Roman society in verse satire unfolds a story of – and anxiety about – Rome's lost Republican identity, never to be recovered. Thus, satire becomes yet another fruitful avenue of approach to the way the Romans thought about themselves, their society, and the poet's place in that society.

As an urban genre, usually set in the city and obsessed with the pretensions and ills of urban lifestyle, what can satire tell us about gardens? At the most basic level, Horace and Juvenal easily fold into the urban landscape of satire the Gardens of Caesar on the Janiculum (Horace *Satire* 1.9.18), the gardens of Lucan (Juvenal 7.79-80), and the gardens of Seneca (Juvenal 10.16-17). For the moralizing satirist, the city – dangerous, unhealthy, pretentious – provides an endless source of outrage and a foil for the discourse of the 'good old days' (see Braund 1989 for an excellent discussion of the antithesis between city and country in Roman satire). As part of the landscape of the Roman literary imagination, gardens mentioned in satire iterate this dialectic between city and country and are integrated into the discourse of immorality.

While the moral dichotomy between city and country is portrayed as clear-cut, the morality of gardens is not so black and white. Gardens remind city dwellers of a better life in the country; they are retreats from the ills of urban decay, places where contact with the soil and the elements refreshes the soul. Horace rejoices in the simplicity of his Sabine farm, whose chief delight was its garden: 'This was what I prayed for: a modest measure of land, nothing big, where there would be a garden, and a spring of ever-flowing water near the house, and a woods a little beyond that' (*Satire* 2.6.1-3). *Hortus*, in the singular, carries positive moral connotations. On the other hand, as we have seen, urban *horti* in the plural are not to be confused with the simple kitchen garden of a farm house. The gardens in the city of Rome were not created for produce but for pleasure and the extravagant display of wealth. Juvenal lists gardens among the many ill-gotten gains of the wealthy (1.75-6, *hortos*) and Horace describes how the recently bankrupt businessman Damasippus lost his fortune by attempting to profit from trading real estate, in the form of pleasure gardens (*Satire* 2.3.24, *hortos*). Since gardening is predicated on weeding out undesirable elements, Horace can deploy the metaphor of weeding when advising a friend to examine his own character for flaws that must be purged: 'for in neglected fields grows coarse bracken that must be burnt' (*Satire* 1.3.37; the Neronian satirist Persius makes 'bracken' a vulgar metaphor at 4.41). Thus, as satire is obsessed with social hierarchy and the distasteful transgressions of strictly imposed boundaries, so the garden makes a logical symbol.

Horace idealizes the repose of his Sabine farm, contrasting it to the vices and anxieties of city life. In particular, he points to the endless round of business conducted by his patron Maecenas at his residence on the Esquiline hill in Rome (*Satire* 2.6.32-4): 'But as soon as I arrive at the gloomy Esquiline, a hundred tasks that don't even concern me jump into my head and beset me on every side.' The Gardens of Maecenas were located on this gloomy Esquiline, built over what had once been the site of a large communal burial ground. The poetics – and politics – of the Gardens of Maecenas will occupy us for the rest of this chapter.

In what follows (as in what preceded), the terms 'politics' and 'political' are taken to encompass not merely governmental administration and associated activities, but in a broader sense that refers to

38

a range of activities that control the distribution and flow of power in a society. In this strong reading, I follow Habinek's lead: 'More than just a common discourse through which issues can be discussed and values negotiated, although it is that as well, Latin literature constitutes a crucial site of contest over the distribution of power in the Roman world as well as a social practice with real historical consequences of its own' (1998, 8). It is no coincidence that both Habinek and Finlay (quoted at the beginning of the Introduction) style Latin literature and gardens, respectively, as sites of contest.

II

In *Satire* 1.8, a statue of the god Priapus in the Gardens of Maecenas tells his story. He begins by recounting his construction from the trunk of a fig tree and by recalling that the gardens where he resides used to be a paupers' cemetery. His job is to ward off thieves and pests from the garden, but he is particularly menaced by the old hags who still come to the former burial grounds to practise their black magic and necromancy. One night, he saw Canidia and Sagana dig a trench in the earth and fill it with the blood of a black lamb; they employed voodoo dolls and invoked the dread deities of the underworld, all before Priapus' very eyes. He stood immobile and unable to stop them, until he farted so loudly that he split his fig-wood buttocks and frightened the witches out of the garden. They ran off, one dropping her false teeth, the other her wig, and both losing their herbs and magic bracelets along the way. The fifty-line poem ends with a joke and a laugh.

Satire 1.8 generates some pressing methodological questions. Normally, when reading any poetry, the reader must come to terms with the speaker, the 'I' of a poem: First, is the subject the actual, historical poet, or is it a voice through which the poet speaks? This leads to the next question, are the events related in a poem actual historical events, or the creations of the poet's imagination? Satire is especially difficult because the speaker of the poem, who often reveals biographical details about his life, also expresses criticism so strident that it would make his character, if real, most irksome. Furthermore, satire is riddled with contradictions; the satirist often partakes of the very behaviour he so vehemently deplores. So in *Satire* 1.9, the upwardly mobile Horace tells of his encounter with a social climber who will not leave him alone. The meaning of a satirical poem is constantly under-cut by irony and humour. Yet this self-denigrating style proves a very effective construct for satirical tone. In satire, solid ground (the hall-mark of a garden) is swept away, so to speak.

In an attempt to reconcile the problem of the shifting subject of satire, Oliensis mines the 'I' statements not for the information they reveal about Horace's extrapoetic life but for what they can tell us about 'the life that happens in his poetry' (Oliensis 1998, 3). While such an approach surmounts the methodological impasse, it must not be taken to extremes. It is too easy to talk about a Horatian poetics separate from the material circumstances of poetic production, thereby enervating the political force of his poetry. At some point, the Horace of the poems intersects with the Horace of historical fact (see e.g. Nisbet 1984), even if that intersection is regularly, indeed system-atically, hidden from full view. Rather than conquer the problem, the reader of satire must embrace the blind spot – or at least come to expect it.

With that said, we derive most of what we know about Horace from his poetry. He was born in 65 BCE in the rural south of Italy at Venusia, 'uncertain whether a Lucanian or Apulian' (*Satire* 2.1.34). His father was an ex-slave who had become an auction agent (see Fraenkel 1957, 4-5). Upon completing his education at Rome and Athens, he joined the retinue of Brutus, one of the assassins of Julius Caesar in 44 BCE. When he returned to Italy after the battle of Philippi, he discovered that his land had been confiscated. He shrewdly took a position as a secretary in the office of public finances, a post that offered him a comfortable income and a smart new set of friends (*Epistles* 2.2.41-57). Vergil and Varius introduced their friend Horace to Maecenas, the man who was to become his patron and give him his Sabine farm (*Satire* 1.6.45-64, 2.6.41-2). Through Maecenas, Horace gained access to Augustus, who eventually invited the poet to accept a position on his staff.

The voice of *Satire* 1.8 is especially compelling, for the speaker in the poem is not the historical Horace, nor the poet Horace; it is not even the god himself, but an icon, a *statue* of the god Priapus. In poems where Priapus resides in a garden or orchard as a watchman, the god makes clear, according to Parker (1988, 6), 'that he has a "master" who

40

has "set him up" and to whom he owes fealty'. In *Satire* 1.8, Priapus is
set up by Maecenas, to whom Horace likewise owes fealty. Although
the *Priapea* doubtless postdates Horace's *Satires*, nevertheless it is
likely that Horace must have had a 'Priapean poetic tradition on which
to draw' (Hallett 1981, 345n.18). Thus, while Horace may not owe a
direct debt to the *Priapea*, nonetheless *Satire* 1.8 shares all of the
characteristics of this collection of poems which take as their subject
the ithyphallic god and his duty to protect boundaries and ward off
intruders. With Horace as author and the statue of Priapus as
speaker, *Satire* 1.8 offers two simultaneous opportunities to observe
the levels of awareness of the garden's transgressive and transformative effects. At what point does it appear that the poet Horace and the
speaker Priapus, whether in separate registers or more likely in voice
melded together, are awakened to their own presence in the poem?

III

From the outset, Priapus is self-consciously iconic. In fact, he begins
not with a statement of his existence as a statue, but with a statement
of his former existence as a shapeless piece of wood that sounds
remarkably like Columella's later description of the Priapus statue
(10.31-4). Horace's Priapus, however, specifies exactly what type of
wood he is hewn from: 'Once I was the trunk of a fig tree, worthless
wood, until a craftsman, unsure as to whether he should fashion a
bench or a Priapus, preferred to make the god. So, I am a god, quite
the terror to thieves and birds, for my right hand checks (*coercet*)
thieves, as does this red pole (*palus*) sticking straight up from my
sinister groin' (*Satire* 1.8.1-5). Then, foreshadowing the impotence of
this *palus* (a Latin word that phonologically, at any rate, approximates the Greek *phallos*), Priapus describes his other threatening
feature: 'the reed stuck on the top of my head frightens the troublesome kites and keeps them from settling in these new gardens' (*Satire*
1.8.6-7). In a poem that takes place in a garden, *coercet*, 'checks', is a
loaded verb whose semantic range extends from the general notion of
checking or restraining, to the more specific pruning, bringing into
order, and eventually punishing.

    After this introduction, Priapus continues to describe his setting: 'A
fellow slave used to bargain for a plot for the corpses that were tossed

41

out from their narrow slave cubicles to be carried in a cheap coffin to this place. This used to be a pauper's grave for the wretched common folk, for the rake Pantolabus and Nomentanus his spendthrift grandson. Here was a boundary stone used to measure a plot a thousand feet in front, three hundred feet deep, and on it was the injunction, "This monument is not to descend to the heirs" ' (1.8.8-13). With the measurement of its boundaries and the declaration of its rules, it would seem that the metamorphosis of the graveyard into garden is begun; however, as we shall see, the transformation is by no means complete or irreversible.

Indeed, the very next lines announce a more precise location for this garden: 'Now one can dwell on the healthful Esquiline and promenade along the sunny embankment, where only recently folk, depressed by the sight, used to look at a field foul with white bones' (1.8.14-16). A third-century BCE inscription from the Italian town of Luceria in Apulia records the *Lex Lucerina*, a law prohibiting the dumping of refuse, the abandoning of corpses, and the performance of sacrifices in honour of the dead. In his in-depth study of this law, Bodel argues that the legal status of the Esquiline burial ground in Rome was determined not by religious considerations, but by matters of public health (1994, 38-54). As one can imagine, mass graves, according to Hopkins' rather gruesome description, were extremely unpleasant (1983, 207-11). When it came to burial, Romans were no doubt deeply concerned with sanitation. From the inscriptions recording prohibitions against creating dumping grounds for refuse and corpses (like the *Lex Lucerina*) found in Rome in the region of the Esquiline, it is evident that illegal disposal of bodies in this area was a serious problem (Bodel 1994, 44; Purcell 1987a, 37). Maecenas did a great service to the city by converting this paupers' graveyard into a luxury garden.

The bones of the dead triggered an image that continued to haunt Horace. In the pessimistic *Epode* 16 (usually dated to 31-29 BCE, although perhaps earlier), Horace bemoans the destruction of Rome under civil war. As Rome is sacked, the conqueror will trample the city with clattering hooves and unearth the grave of the legendary hero Quirinus; his bones will be scattered (16.11-14). The white bones of bygone graveyards were to become a recurring, horrific image of transformation in Latin literature. Propertius closes his first book of

42

poetry with two ten-line elegies that address the aftermath of Rome's recent civil war. A grieving sister will find her brother's bones scattered on Etruscan hillsides (1.21.9-10); the bones of those slaughtered at Perusia lie unburied (1.22.6-8). Taken up by Vergil in his description of the battlefields in the coastal plain between the south bend of the Tiber and the city of Latinus, where 'great plains grow white with bones' (*Aeneid* 12.36), this image of white bones is echoed later by Tacitus in his recollection of the defeat of Varus and his three legions in the Teutoburg forest in 9 CE (*Annals* 1.61.2, *albentia ossa*). In his rendition of this Tacitean episode, the modern poet Frank Bidart fully comprehends the power of the image and twice repeats the whitening bones as symbols of return (Bidart 1997).

Before the *Aeneid* and the *Annals*, however, the bones of decayed corpses in *Satire* 1.8 and *Epode* 16 may have found a place in Vergil's earlier poem, the *Georgics*. Vergil predicts that one day, a farmer ploughing a field will inadvertently unearth the weapons, helmets, and bones of the slain (*Georgics* 1.497). For both Horace and later Vergil, the earth has the power to restore fertility from death. The whitening bones are symbols of transformation from cemetery to garden, from battlefield to grain field. The transformation completes a cycle of land use. War, death, and destruction are seen as only temporary; the white bones symbolize the redemption of the killing fields. We shall return to this cycle of transformation that adumbrates an anxiety over one of the most disruptive transformations in the landscape, for in the years between the assassination of Julius Caesar and the decisive Battle of Actium (the so-called triumviral years, 44-31 BCE), land throughout the Italian peninsula was confiscated and re-allotted.

The bones in the garden are a problem for Priapus, for their sterility (as opposed to his over-determined fertility) attracts not the regular thieves in search of rich produce (as, for example, plump, juicy pears will tempt Augustine to theft, as we shall see in Chapter 4) or wild beasts in search of prey, but 'those who practise on human souls with spells and poisons. I cannot destroy or ward them off in any way, for as soon as the errant moon brings forth a full, lovely face, they come collecting bones and pernicious herbs' (1.8.19-22). Priapus does not name his most troublesome enemy, but he does offer a revealing clue, evident in the Latin, if not in the English translation. The pronouns

43

are feminine; these creatures who haunt his garden under a full moon are distinctively female (not surprisingly so; see Newman 1998 on Horace's deliberate choice of women as the target of invective poetry).

From the general, Priapus launches into a specific tale of two particular witches on one particular night: 'I myself saw Canidia, her black robe tucked up, walking barefoot with her hair unbound, howling along with the elder Sagana; their complexions made both horrible to behold. They began to scratch the earth with their nails' (mocking the hoe and mattock?) 'and to rip apart a dark lamb with their teeth. The blood was poured into the trench so that they might summon the shades of the dead, souls to answer questions' (1.8.23-9). The ritual in literature is as old as Homer: Odysseus poured out blood to summon spirits from the Underworld. To be sure, Canidia and Sagana are not epic heroines, nor is their quest noble.

Canidia and Sagana adhere to some of the basic rules of gendered discourse. First, 'woman' is a definitional tool that operates as the opposite of 'man' (Archer, Fischler, and Wyke 1994, xvii; Skinner 1997, 8). The witches, female and profane, are the opposite of the hyper-masculine, sacred Priapus. Secondly, they illustrate one of the fundamental principles of Roman gendered discourse, that whenever women usurp power, they constitute a threat that must be controlled. Thirdly, Roman satirists notoriously exaggerate women's sexual misconduct. Political invective can deploy adultery as a weapon against women; the tropes of satire reinforce the stereotypical sexual deviance of women (Richlin 1992; Edwards 1993, 35-6, 57). In keeping with the ironic mode of satire, the witches, however, are sexually impotent. They are old and devoid of any alluring charms. Their whole purpose for being in the cemetery is to deploy magic against an unrequited love. Fourthly, there is a tension between the specific portrayal of these two individual witches, Sagana and Canidia in particular (for she also appears in other poems of Horace, as we shall see) and a stereotype of evil witches, for example, Medea. Finally and quintessentially, Canidia and Sagana demonstrate the tendency of Roman satire to be engrossed with departures from the established norms (cf. Skinner 1997, 5). Witches are anomalies both sexually and morally, socially and religiously, and these irregularities serve as symbolic frameworks for identifying and denigrating the fundamental nature of women.

44

2. The Garden of Politics

In a study of invective against women in Roman satire, Richlin explores the stereotype of the old, repulsive woman. 'In fact,' she argues, 'old women evoke the most intense expressions of fear and disgust, along with a sense that they constitute a sort of uncanny other' (Richlin 1984, 71). The 'old woman' is generally the opposite of a mother or a *matrona*. An old woman is often an advisor who leads well-meaning youngsters astray or a witch who can not only charm, but whose potions, abortifacients and poisons, subvert the traditional female functions of nurturing and reproduction (Richlin 1984, 72). Thus the witches in *Satire* 1.8 conform to the stereotype of old women as deviants (on Horace's skill and ingenuity in reworking various aspects of the ageing-women theme, see Esler 1989). Furthermore, in their ability to communicate with both living and dead, the witches transgress and defy one of the most fundamental boundaries of human existence.

The herbs grown in gardens possess a dangerous duality, for they can be used as legitimate, healing medicines, but they can also be used to concoct deadly poisons. Pharmacology is attested in Homer, who makes a distinction between healing and toxic drugs. In folklore and in history, the concoction and administering of toxins is often attributed to women. Perhaps the most famous poisoner was Locusta, pharmacist to the Julio-Claudians. She was employed by Agrippina the Younger to poison Claudius, and by Nero against Britannicus. Long before Locusta, however, women had been preparing poisons in Rome; according to Livy (8.18), in the year 331 BCE, one hundred and seventy women were found guilty of preparing and administering poisons to the leading citizens of Rome.

With its condemnation of secret witchcraft rituals and the expulsion of the witches from the garden, *Satire* 1.8 also calls to mind the events of 186 BCE. During the famed Bacchanalian conspiracy, the consuls were charged with investigating the practices of the cult and the widespread worship of Bacchus throughout the Italian peninsula. In response, the Senate issued a decree that dismantled the large-scale worship. In his novelistic account of the conspiracy, Livy reports that an unwilling witness, Hispala (a former slave woman), discloses the secret rituals of the Bacchanalia: 'When someone is initiated, he is handed over to priests just like a sacrificial victim; they lead him to a place which resounds with shrieks and the music of instruments and

45

the blasts of cymbals and drums, to drown out his shouts crying out as
he is raped violently' (39.10.7). Just as Priapus unwillingly witnesses
and then discloses the witches' secret rites in the garden, so Hispala
unwillingly witnesses and then discloses the secret rites of the Bacchanalia; both are vehicles by which the author may describe
frightening, unholy rituals and speak the unspeakable. The involve-
ment of women in the cult, together with charges of poisoning, added
to the general climate of hysteria. In the next chapter, we shall see
that the mania – and phobia – of Bacchic worship persisted deep into
the Julio-Claudian era, when the empress Messalina played the part
of a bacchic maenad during a masquerade of the annual vintage
celebration.

   In addition to the distant historical events of 331 and 186 BCE, the
contemporary climate in Rome may have played into Horace's imagination when creating the witches of *Satire* 1.8. In 33 BCE, two years
after the publication of this poem, Agrippa, although of consular rank,
took on the burdensome duties of the much lower office of aedile, or
public custodian, and performed many public services at his own
expense. He repaired public buildings and streets, cleaned out the
sewers, distributed olive oil and salt, and provided the baths free of
charge throughout the year for both men and women. Dio appends to
this list a final act of euergetism: Agrippa drove the astrologers and
magicians from the city (Dio 49.43.5). Again in 29 BCE, Agrippa is
supposed to have advised Octavian to punish atheists, sorcerers, and
those who distort religion with strange rites, asserting that from
foreign practices spring up conspiracies (Dio 52.36.1-3). Perhaps Horace's poem responds to the preponderance of pernicious witchcraft
that Agrippa eventually expels from the city (Lejay 1966, 220). Manning goes so far as to argue that Horace's knowledge of the rites and
rituals, evident in his detailed descriptions in both *Satire* 1.8 and
Epodes 5 and 17, may have come from contact with such actual
'back-street' people (Manning 1970, 394).

   One need not conjecture about the historical realities of magic in
Rome in the 30s BCE. Plenty of witches abound in mythology to fuel
Horace's poetic imagination. In the *Odyssey*, Circe transforms Odysseus' men into pigs, but Odysseus resists her magic, thanks to the
power of a herb given by Hermes. Perhaps the most famous witch of
classical mythology is Medea, daughter of Aeëtes, king of Colchis. She

falls in love with Jason, provides him with a magic potion to protect him as he completes the king's dangerous tasks, and charms the dragon that guarded the golden fleece. Upon returning to Jason's native Iolcus, Medea rejuvenates his ageing father with a magic potion. When betrayed by her husband, Medea sends a robe and crown dipped in deadly poison to Jason's mistress Creusa. At every turn, Medea relies on powerful herbs to create potions, charms, and poisons.

Indeed, the archetypical Medea serves Horace's purposes well. Canidia is first introduced in a rather harmless aside in *Epodes* 3, where she is compared to Medea. Again in *Epode* 5, Canidia laments the failure of the potions she learned from Medea (5.61-2). In his first-century CE rendition of the tragedy *Medea*, Seneca the Younger describes the witch collecting herbs:

> When she had summoned forth the whole race of snakes, she gathered an evil store of baleful herbs. Whatever grows on the rocks of trackless Eryx, plants that grow on heights clothed in unbroken winter, the heights of Caucasus, spattered with Prometheus' gore; plants with which the rich Arabians smear their arrows, and the bold Mede, girt with his quiver, or the light-armed Parthians; or those juices which, under the cold pole, high-born Sueban women gather in the Hyrcanian groves; whatever the earth produces in the nest-building springtime or when frozen winter has stripped the woods of their glory and bound all things with icy fetters; all plants that bloom with deadly flower, and all whose juices breed cause of death in their twisted roots – all these she handles (*Medea* 705-19).

Deadly herbs, it seems, are grown at the edges of the Roman world (Arabia, Parthia, and Hyrcania, farthest east of all). The encyclopaedic quality of this catalogue mimics similar lists in the Roman agricultural literature of Cato, Varro, and Pliny the Elder, where the garden encapsulates the far reaches of the Roman empire within its borders. Plants from around the world represent a terrestrial totality. Likewise, Medea gathers herbs from across the globe, demonstrating her imperial command of magic. Steeped in both historical and mythological antecedents, Canidia and Sagana in *Satire* 1.8 and their threat of poison conjure some of the most deep-seated and long standing fears and anxieties among Roman men: the threats posed by old women with secret powers, and knowledge of dark arts coupled with a command of pharmacology in particular.

Returning to our reading of *Satire* 1.8, we find that Canidia and Sagana continue their sinister rites by producing effigies, a larger one of wool placed as if to inflict punishment over a smaller one of wax that stood in its torment like a slave about to die. One witch called for Hecate, the other for dire Tisiphone. Priapus is helpless to stop the rites and helpless to escape them: 'You would have seen the snakes and hounds of hell unleashed and the red moon hide behind great tombs rather than witness these deeds' (1.8.34-6). The immobility that makes Priapus vulnerable also makes him a credible witness. Other creatures more accustomed to such foul deeds cannot bear the sight that Priapus must behold. He goes on to validate his testimony: 'If I am lying about any of this, may the white shit of ravens mess my head and may Iulius, frail Pediatia, and the thief Voranus come upon me to piss and shit' (1.8.37-9). A fine promise, since stationary statues are always the target of crows and nasty boys anyway. The scatological nature of these lines prepares us for the grand finale. Before concluding, however, Priapus asks one more question, whereby he ends up relating the very deeds he thinks are unspeakable: 'Why should I recount in detail?' (1.8.40). Sagana asks the shades questions; they respond; the witches bury a wolf's head and a snake's tooth; they throw the waxen doll in the fire to make it blaze. Once again the authority of Priapus as witness rests on his capacity to speak, as Agamben says, 'solely in the name of an incapacity to speak' (Agamben 1999, 158). This helplessness is precisely what gives Priapus the authority to describe rituals best left in the dark.

When taken by itself, the magic performed in *Satire* 1.8 may seem as harmless as a teenage girl's slumber party séance; however, these rituals acquire a much more disturbing tone because Canidia surfaces elsewhere in the poetry of Horace, where her magic is much more violent and disturbing. In *Epode* 5, a boy is kidnapped by a band of witches who prepare to torture him to death and turn parts of him into a love potion. The leader Canidia prays to her gods and explains that her previous love potions failed. The boy curses the witches and promises that his ghost will haunt them; he predicts that a mob will stone them and leave their bodies for scavengers. It is interesting to note that in *Epode* 5, the witches gather wood for their purification rites, cypress trees and 'goat fig' (*caprificos*, 5.17); so perhaps the fig-wood Priapus of *Satire* 1.8 has a legitimate fear of witches. At the end of the poem, the witches' bones will be ravaged by 'Esquiline wolves and carrion birds' (5.99-100), proof that the transformation of the Esquiline from pauper's graveyard to stately garden is still not complete. In *Epode* 17, the final poem in the *Epode* book, the poet pleads with Canidia to stop torturing him; he is willing to admit her powers. The witch, however, is relentless and says that for his crimes, the poet will be punished until he begs in vain for death. The poet is willing to bear witness to her power and no longer has trouble speaking of her abilities, unlike the unwilling Priapus.

As *Satire* 1.8 comes to a conclusion, Priapus shudders at the words and deeds of these witches, but he is a witness soon to be avenged (*non testis inultus*, 1.8.44). 'With a sound like a burst bladder, I farted and my buttocks of fig-wood split asunder. They ran to the city, Canidia dropping her teeth and Sagana her wig along the way, losing their herbs and love-knot bracelets: You would have seen the whole thing and laughed and laughed' (1.8.46-50). At the end of the poem, Priapus returns to his sense of self as a fig-wood icon and is awakened from his garden reverie. Although for a time carried away by the evil rituals, in the end he regains consciousness. According to Elkins, something about gardens transforms those who describe them, inducing a trance-like mode that abandons rational analysis and revels in the moment. Priapus, overwhelmed by the magic performed before his very eyes, is recalled to his duty as protector even as he is physically transformed. The explosive ending of the poem reminds the reader that conventions are at work: the talking statue is but a wooden object; the poem is but a written document.

This loud, obnoxious fart that brings *Satire* 1.8 to a close has embarrassed readers for centuries. Although scholars do not blush to theorize on such sensitive subjects as intercourse, rape, sodomy, and pederasty, few consider farting a fruitful avenue of inquiry into Roman social relations. Passing gas is of course a standard feature of ancient comedy, and so it adds yet another component to the generic medley that characterizes satire. In *Satire* 1.8, there is no hint that the Gardens of Maecenas, a former graveyard, is a sweet-smelling place. The embarrassment caused by Horace's overtly distasteful

expression distracts the reader from more potent possibilities of interpretation. According to Barthes (1976, 137), 'Language has this
property of denying, ignoring, dissociating reality: when written, shit
does not have an odour.' To my mind, Horace's language at the end of
Satire 1.8 works twice as hard as Barthes would have it. On the one
hand, language operates in such a way that one's nose is never
actually offended by the word *pepedi*. Although the reduplicated perfect tense is coyly onomatopoeic, still when left untranslated, its sense
of odour is further distanced. On the other hand, *pepedi* sets into
motion a whole new level of denial, disregard, and dissociation. I
believe that the poem expresses an anxiety over a rapidly transforming landscape whose transformations only serve to trigger further
transgressions; however, Horace obscures this disturbing political
worry in a cloud of flatulence. While the fart is probably the most
memorable part of the poem, attention to the setting of the poem in
the Gardens of Maecenas brings out the themes of transgression and
transformation that make this poem a powerful statement of Horatian
poetics – and politics.

IV

Behind Priapus and Canidia, behind the sexual aggression and the
magic, behind all that transpires in *Satire* 1.8, looms the figure of
Maecenas, owner of the garden – and Horace's friend and patron.
Maecenas was among Octavian's earliest and most constant supporters, in an alliance that began as early as the battle of Philippi in 42
BCE. He is also one of the most unusual men of the age. Never elected
a magistrate, never a member of the Senate, the equestrian Maecenas
was nevertheless a most intimate and trusted friend and agent of
Octavian, representing him at the precarious negotiations of the
treaties of Brundisium and Tarentum. Twice Octavian left him in
charge of Rome and Italy in his absence; for precedence for this most
unusual 'office', Tacitus had to hark all the way back to the days of the
legendary kings, when Romulus, Tullus Hostilius, and Tarquinius
Superbus appointed temporary officials when they left Rome (*Annals*
6.11). Upon his death in 8 BCE, Maecenas bequeathed his entire estate
to Augustus, including his magnificent house and gardens on the
Esquiline. He is the dedicatee of Vergil's *Georgics* and mentioned as a

patron by Propertius. To Maecenas, Horace dedicated his first book of *Satires*, the *Epodes*, the first three books of *Odes*, and the first book of *Epistles*. Whatever the poets may have owed to Maecenas, he provided them a unique service, for according to Griffin (1984, 195), 'the relationship with Maecenas could serve the poets as a smoked glass, as it were, between them and the naked glare of the sun of Augustus'. Maecenas was a powerful man, but because he held no office, he could not formally be charged with responsibility for the successes or failures of the emerging regime.

Satire 1.8 suggests that Maecenas did the citizens of Rome a favour when he built his magnificent garden estate. Located on the edge of the city of Rome, the Gardens of Maecenas are peripheral, both physically and metaphorically. The plateau of the Esquiline was included within the wall of Servius, the early Republican fortification of the city. This wall forms the *agger*, or the embankment along which Priapus suggests it is now pleasant to stroll. This wall gives the Esquiline a sense of boundary, which is compounded by the Gardens of Maecenas along the edge. In addition, because it is transformed from a cemetery, the transitional status of the Gardens of Maecenas is further underscored. The prowling witches reveal that the transformation is incomplete, for they can still threaten the peace of the garden by conjuring its former status as a cemetery. No longer a cemetery for the witches to inhabit, but not yet completely transformed into a garden for Priapus to protect, the Gardens of Maecenas in *Satire* 1.8 cannot be defined in absolutes.

The difference between a garden and a graveyard was, and still is to some extent, fluid, adding another dimension to the poem's ambivalent setting. Like a garden, a cemetery is one of the most significant – and permanent – ways social status is manifested. For the wealthy, a sterile pleasure garden is a way to display status; for the poor, the produce of a vegetable garden is a vital means of sustenance. For the wealthy, funerary monuments record in inscriptions or recreate in sculpture the life of the deceased; the poor are lucky to be covered with a handful of dirt. Thus the social function of gardens and of cemeteries intersect; both are places where status is deeply embedded in the landscape. Many wealthy aristocrats were buried in garden settings (Purcell 1987a, 31). The mausoleum of Augustus was set in a garden, and the tombs of Caligula and Nero were located in the Gardens of

Lamianus and Domitia. Cicero's daughter was laid to rest in a garden, and the poet Lucan was buried in a garden with statues. The curious blend of garden and cemetery fascinated Lady Emmeline Wortley upon her visit in 1849 to the newly created Mount Auburn Cemetery in Cambridge, Massachusetts. She eloquently describes the confluence of garden and graveyard:

> The finely diversified grounds occupy about one hundred acres, in general profusely adorned with a rich variety of trees, and in some places planted with ornamental shrubbery: there are some tombs graced with charming flower beds. There are also some pretty sheets of water there: it is divided into different avenues and paths, which have various names. Generally they are called after the trees or flowers that abound there, such as lily, poplar, cypress, violet, woodbine, and others. It is, indeed, a beauteous city for the dead. The birds were singing most mellifluously and merrily – it was quite a din of music that they kept up in these solemn but lovely shades. ... There are some graceful and well-executed monuments within its precincts (Wortley 1868, 47-8).

Garden and cemetery are not mutually exclusive sites. The nineteenth-century scientist Jacob Bigelow describes the process of transformation at Mount Auburn:

> In a few years, when the hand of taste shall have scattered among the trees, as it has already begun to do, enduring memorials of marble and granite, a landscape of the most picturesque character will be created. No place in the environs of our city will possess stronger attractions to the visitor. To the mourner it offers seclusion amid the consoling influences of nature (Bigelow 1859, 197).

Both Mount Auburn and the Gardens of Maecenas were transformed from cemetery to garden; however, in neither case was the transformation ever complete.

Set on the margins of the city, the Gardens of Maecenas further marginalize the social outcasts that inhabit it, the old hags and the rustic Priapus. Such an ambivalent setting, where the boundaries between city and country, death and life are so unstable, invites transgression. Imbued with such polarities, the Gardens of Maecenas involve a battle of oppositions: male versus female, good versus evil, sacred versus profane, even self versus community, if we consider the benefit that Maecenas' personal display of wealth has for the larger community. Such polarity and antithesis (e.g., Francis and Hester 1990, 4) characterize the rhetoric of the garden and drive the rhetoric of transgression at the heart of Horace's poem.

V

Many have tried to explain this anomalous poem – the shortest of the satires, the only one in which a statue speaks – in a variety of ways, all of which tastefully avoid focusing too much attention on the embarrassing ending. For Fraenkel, *Satire* 1.8 introduces a fresh theme to add variety; arguing that it was one of the last poems of the book to be written, Fraenkel is content to conclude that the Priapus poem neatly rounds off the number of poems in the book to ten (1957, 124). Rudd imaginatively posits the poem as an etiology that explains an oddly shaped statue of Priapus that Horace may have seen in the Gardens of Maecenas (1966, 72). Like Rudd, Coffey also says the poem is etiological, explaining the origin of the gardens (1976, 78-9). For McGann, the poem demonstrates the place of coarse and vulgar humour in Horace's poetic hierarchy (1973, 87). Anderson concludes that the poem recapitulates the central themes of the book in patently comic form (1982, 81). After demonstrating that the word 'fig' would have had unmistakable associations with the anus deformed by penile penetration, Hallett finds literary models in the *Priapea* for the poem's fundamental anomaly: whereas Priapus is supposed to assault the anus of the intruder with his penis, in *Satire* 1.8 he assaults the intruders with his fig-wood anus. The passive organ is made active, and serves in lieu of the phallus (Hallett 1981).

Form, purpose, position in the book; a political and polemical interpretation would have to wait for DuQuesnay's assertion that *Satires* 1 promotes the conservatism of the ascending Octavian. In writing *Satires* 1, Horace tries to allay the fears and anxieties of his contemporaries about the intentions, ambitions, and moral character of the new leaders (DuQuesnay 1984, 57). Horace attempts to per-

53

suade others that his friends are trustworthy, and he bases this intention on a sincere belief that Octavian is the best possible solution to the crumbling Republic. Of *Satire* 1.8, DuQuesnay argues that it compliments Maecenas for cleaning up the Esquiline and beautifying Rome, a public service to be added to his establishment of a city 'police force', for which the citizens were also grateful. Canidia and Sagana perform rituals associated with the cult of Pythagoras, and there were known Pythagoreans among the supporters of Sextus Pompey, enemy of Octavian. Therefore, *Satire* 1.8 is not only a compliment to the patron Maecenas, but also an expression of relief at the removal of various undesirables from the city and the end of the troublesome Sextus Pompey and his followers (DuQuesnay 1984, 38-9).

DuQuesnay's political reading of *Satires* 1 is at the heart of further interpretations by Braund (1992, 21), who advocates an allegorical reading of 1.8, and Brown (1993, 170) who also believes that the poem is meant to pay a compliment to Maecenas. For Kiernan (1999, 58), *Satire* 1.8, when taken in conjunction with *Epodes* 5 and 17, expresses Horace's dread of a return to civil war and anarchy, and the relapse into barbarism that such a war would bring. Most recently, Welch has offered a political reading of *Satire* 1.8 that takes its cue from the setting of the poem in the Gardens of Maecenas. She demonstrates that the poem 'contains undercurrents of the tension between Horace's poetry and his patron' (2001, 185), that is, the poem enacts yet again the status anxiety that pervades so much of the Horatian corpus. Griffin has no truck with such readings; vehemently denying that such a ridiculously frivolous poem as *Satire* 1.8 could have any political dimension, he insists that the poem does little more than offset excessive respectability with 'a little judiciously chosen impropriety' (1993, 7). My way of thinking about the politics of *Satire* 1.8 has already been foreshadowed by my interpretation of the white bones of the cemetery as a potent symbol of transformation. Although there will be no convincing some, closer attention to the *Epodes* and to Vergil's *Eclogues* will nevertheless inch sceptics like Griffin a little closer towards accepting a political dimension in this playfully irreverent poem.

Contrary to Lyne (1995, 22-30), who argues that, because both *Satires* I and *Epodes* were composed before Actium, they are not political in the same way as Horace's post-Actium poetry, I believe that both the period of composition and the subject matter make the *Epodes* (and *Satires* 1) a highly politically charged book of poetry. Indeed, for Oliensis (1998, 64-5), the whole book of *Epodes* is situated 'on the brink of the battle of Actium' (see also Fitzgerald 1988 and Barchiesi 2001, 141). I want to look not at one specific event that influenced the way the *Epodes* was written, but rather at the overarching political situation that shaped the book. Written and published between 31 and 29 BCE, the *Epodes* belong to the triumviral period, after Brutus and Cassius, the assassins of Julius Caesar, had been defeated at Philippi but before the power struggle between Antony and Octavian was decided at Actium – and before the full import of that battle was made manifest.

In tone and content, the *Epodes* reflects the emotional impact that this time of brutal sieges and massacres (at Mutina in 43 and Perusia in 41) and frail treaties and pacts (at Brundisium in 40 and Tarentum in 37) had on the psyche of contemporary Romans. According to Mankin (1995, 6), 'it is clear ... that, as a whole, the *Epode* book was meant as a "response" to the crisis of the end of the Republic'. *Epode* 7 asks why fellow citizens rush to civil war. *Epode* 9 expresses the hesitancy of the era and asks when it will be safe to celebrate the victory at Actium. *Epode* 16 bemoans another generation ground down in civil war and advocates abandoning Rome altogether for an unattainable Golden Age. In this response to the optimistic and incipient Golden Age of Vergil's *Eclogue* 4, Horace opts for a utopia, in the etymological sense of the word: a place nowhere to be found.

Perched at the crossroads of *Satire* 1.8 and the book of *Epodes* hovers Canidia. In *Satire* 1.8, *Epode* 5, and 17 she is a major character; in *Epode* 3, *Satire* 2.1, and 2.8 she is mentioned by name. She is possibly alluded to in *Epode* 8 and 12, invective poems against an unnamed old woman who shares many of the baneful features of the uncanny Canidia. From the poems, it is possible to patch together a general description of this vile woman. Canidia resides near and frequents the region of the Esquiline Hill. She appears to be a Roman matron with a husband and children. She is old, ugly, nearly toothless, and has bad breath. She has many lovers, including the poet. She also has followers of her cult with whom she practises her poisoning, love magic, and necromancy. In her dark arts, however, she is not always successful.

55

Two avenues of interpretation beckon our understanding of Canidia. Either she stands for a historical person, or she is a fictional, stock figure with symbolic significance. Taking the first line of interpretation, Rudd (1966, 148) explores the possibilities: Canidia may be constructed on the basis of a group of witches; she may hint at an individual belonging to a group; she may in fact be constructed on the basis of an individual. According to Horace's antique commentator, Porphyrio, Canidia's real name was Gratidia (Porphyrio on *Epode* 3.7), and Horace disguises the name of this woman under a pseudonym (cf. Fraenkel 1957, 62). Even if this were the case, there still remains the possibility that Canidia is simultaneously emblematic. The etymology of her name may provide a clue. Mankin (1995, 300) lists the various possible derivations of her name. Some suggestions are rather far-fetched; for example, 'goose' meaning a rapacious bird, or 'empty', as in false shape. The name may mean 'dog' as in the dog star, which saps men of their virility (Oliensis 1991, 1998, 72-3). Perhaps the name Canidia is related to *canus* meaning 'white or grey-haired', and by extension, 'old age', by which she represents the senescence of Rome and its ancient curse of fratricide (see Anderson 1982, 80-1 on the witches' devotion to a dead, destructive past). Finally, Canidia may represent Rome herself, a woman who lures her lovers and then poisons them with hatred of their fellow citizens.

The Canidia of *Satire* 1.8 foreshadows the witch that soon dominates the politically driven *Epodes*. Therefore, her appearance in *Satire* 1.8 cannot be wholly innocent. With her, Priapus expels from the garden all that is undesirable, sexually, socially – and politically. Symbolically, Priapus drives off the bugbear of civil war and grotesque warfare. As the mass burial ground is transformed into a garden, so the Republic is transformed by the triumvirate, from civil war to reconciliation. *Satire* 1.8 reflects a diffidence in the permanence of that transformation. Just as the garden still bears the bones of its former existence, so one need not scratch too deep beneath the surface of the new order to find the skeletons of civil war. Rather than look forward in the Horatian corpus to the *Epodes* for confirmation of the political meaning adumbrated in *Satire* 1.8, we do well to look sideways, at Horace's contemporary Vergil, and especially at the *Eclogues* to which *Epode* 16 responds so poignantly.

The book which we call *Eclogues* was written and published earlier in the triumviral period, between 42 and 37 BCE. Although the precise order of composition and dating of the ten poems is still controversial (see the exchanges between Bowersock 1971, Clausen 1972, Tarrant 1978, and Bowersock 1978), nevertheless it is possible and probable that the collection appeared before the publication of Horace's *Satires* 1 in 35 or 34 BCE. Even if we follow Clausen (1972, 203) in dating *Eclogue* 1 to 35, then the *Satires* are at the latest simultaneous and do not predate the *Eclogues*. More generally, both books of poetry are what Osgood (2006, 4-5) considers 'triumviral' literature. Osgood fruitfully reconsiders the relationships and resonances among works of literature usually kept under separate generic categories. Although wide-ranging in their form, content, purpose, and scope, Sallust's *Catilinarian Conspiracy*, *War with Jugurtha,* and *Histories*, Vergil's *Eclogues* and *Georgics*, Horace's *Satires* and *Epodes*, the first book of elegies of Propertius, Nepos' biographies, and Varro's last writings, including the extant *On Agriculture*, were all composed in these years of unprecedented political change. Osgood shows how these works reflect the issues that struck the contemporary imagination about these rapid changes. Triumviral literature demonstrates just how widely these contemporary events were experienced. *Satires* I and the *Eclogues* are part of this dynamic and unique literary milieu.

The friendship of Horace and Vergil is another way to explore the relationship between the *Satires* and *Eclogues*. We may take as an example of friendship with a fellow poet the expressions of his relationship with Tibullus (on the identification of Tibullus in Horace's poetry, see Nisbet and Hubbard 1970, 368) and his criticism, both tacit and overt, of Tibullus' poetics and especially his choice of elegy. According to Putnam, Horace criticizes his friend with subtle humour (Putnam 1972, 88); however, his criticism of Vergil is registered in a noticeably different way.

Vergil twice appears in the poetry of Horace as a traveller. In *Satire* 1.5.40, Vergil belongs to the retinue accompanying Maecenas on a diplomatic journey to Brundisium (Brindisi) in 38 BCE. In *Ode* 1.3, Horace offers a prayer for the safety of the vessel that bears Vergil to Greece in 19. *Ode* 1.24 is a consolation to Vergil on the death of a mutual friend. Long before these occasional poems, however, Horace makes a straightforward judgement about the aesthetics of the *Eclogues* at the end of *Satires* 1: 'Grace and sweetness are Vergil's gifts, from the Muses who love the countryside' (1.10.44-5). Here at the end of his first book of *Satires*, Horace openly acknowledges the influence of a poet whose vestiges can be found throughout the collection.

The *Eclogues* leave their mark on the *Satires* in both form and content. Both are collections of poems that evoke abundance and variety. Like the *Satires* packed full of various delights, the *Eclogues* are an assortment of selected delights. Two of the *Eclogues* close with the notion of abundance and satiety. To end the contest in *Eclogue* 3, the judge Palaemon declares 'the meadows have drunk enough' (*sat prata biberunt*, 3.111), that is, they are sated with poetry. The poet's final endeavour (*extremum ... laborem*, 10.1) ends with an *envoi* that urges, 'go home, full-fed goats, the evening star comes, go home' (*ite domum saturae, venit Hesperus, ite capellae*, 10.77). The poems of the *Eclogues* have filled their purpose.

Furthermore, Leach outlines the correspondences in form between the *Eclogues*, *Satires* 1, and Tibullus' first book of elegies. These three books of ten poems each are of comparable length; they were written within a decade of each other; each was the first major publication of the poet's career; Vergil and Tibullus were both friends of Horace (Leach 1978, 79). According to Leach, each book exhibits the same symmetrical pattern of arrangement, three groups of three poems and a finale. In all three books of poetry, programmatic poems occur at the same interval. All three poets approached their genres in different ways, but all had the common task of self-definition. While the eighth *Eclogue* and *Satire* are both about magic, a common note of disillusionment characterizes the ninth poems (Leach 1978, 95). The final and perhaps most convincing argument that the *Eclogues*, *Satires* 1, and Tibullus 1 are kindred in form (and therefore in content too) is that the variety of other collections suggests that the book of ten poems was scarcely conventionalized (Leach 1978, 100). Such evidence leads to the conclusion that the book of *Eclogues* was a model of design; however, moments in *Satires* 1 betray a resistance to a wholesale acceptance of this model. Just as Horace's poems to Tibullus disclose a strain of criticism of elegy, so Horace finds fault with his other poet friend as well. In the *Satires* of Horace, Zetzel finds both admiration and homage, criticism and revision of his bucolic predecessor (Zetzel 2002, 46). Horace shapes and changes the direction of Vergil's poetry, from a backward nostalgia to a forward-looking poetry.

2. The Garden of Politics

For both the *Eclogues* and the *Satires*, the city is a central preoccupation, although expressed in radically different ways. The pastoral world idealizes a permanently irretrievable rustic world, and in the absence of this lost world pastoral is created by one consigned to an anti-rustic, that is, urban life (see Halperin 1983, 27-35 on the problems of defining pastoral). Thus, as satire privileges the city squarely at the centre of its social critique, so pastoral erases the city altogether and fills its void with an unattainable utopia (so, for example, Halperin 1990 speaks of pastoral as disengaged, inward, and reflective). Both genres thus respond to the irreconcilable problem at the heart of any agricultural society. Once people decide to eat what they plant (instead of eating what they find), then they must come to terms with the permanent results of this decision. Planting, sowing, and basing survival on these acts change the relationship that humankind has with the land. No longer free to gather produce as it is given, humans become tied to the earth and its produce. This haunting loss of freedom colours both pastoral and satire. In many ways, Horace's *Satires* are the other self of Vergil's *Eclogues*. As pastoral effaces the city that caused the permanent loss of a bygone, longed-for, forever unattainable rustic way of life, so satire targets the city that caused that aching loss.

In addition to all these features of form, some specific content of the *Eclogues* also makes its way into the early poetry of Horace (see van Rooy 1973). For example, Lucina the goddess of childbirth appears in the so-called messianic *Eclogue* 4.10 where she presides over the birth of this fortunate child. In *Epode* 5.6, the captive boy tortured at the hands of Canidia swears by Lucina. Perhaps in this poem, Horace responds to the joyful tone of *Eclogue* 4 by invoking its matron goddess in a most horrific setting. In *Eclogue* 7, a statue of Priapus guards a poor garden. 'Now we have made you of marble for the time being; but you will be of gold, if ever births make full the flock' (7.35-6). For Vergil, marble is a poor substance; Horace goes one better and fashions his garden Priapus of fig-wood – a wood that is desirable to witches. In the ten satires of Book 1, Horace responds, whether intentionally or unintentionally, to Vergil's collection of ten pastoral poems (cf. Zetzel 2002, 46).

Beyond these simple associations of form and content, however, lurks a more pressing concern of both poets about the reapportionment of land in the recent confiscations and settlements of Octavian.

On 27 November 43 BCE, the *Lex Titia* established the triumvirate according to the pact at Bononia. Antony, Lepidus, and Octavian divided up the provinces and called themselves *tresviri rei publicae constituendae*, triumvirs for the establishment of the state. Rather than exercise the clemency of Caesar, who strategically pardoned his political enemies, they decided to root out their opponents by proscription, a tactic not employed since the ruthless dictatorship of Sulla in 82. They condemned to death 300 senators and 2,000 knights; Cicero topped the list and was hunted down and killed immediately. Towards family and friends, the triumvirs were particularly ruthless; it was as if they were trying to impress each other in loyalty as much as drive out their political enemies. Although Syme (1939, 191-2) cautions prudence when assessing the carnage, nevertheless the fear of proscription surely hung over all the citizens, regardless of the numbers of actual victims (see Osgood 2006, 62-79 for a balanced and sensitive discussion of the proscriptions).

The proscriptions could not fully replenish the state coffers exhausted by civil war, and Octavian had to pay his soldiers somehow. Civil war did not yield foreign booty, thus payment had to come from fellow citizens. According to the historian Appian, to encourage his army, Octavian promised the soldiers eighteen cities of Italy as colonies; the most famous were Capua, Rhegium, Venusia, Beneventum, Nuceria, Ariminum, and Vibo. 'Thus were the most beautiful parts of Italy marked out for the soldiers' (*Civil Wars* 4.3). The confiscation of land began in earnest after the battle of Philippi and continued for ten years.

Veterans were dissatisfied with the speed of their settlements, and owners threatened by ejection protested and petitioned for the return of their land. In the midst of this turmoil, the *Eclogues* were written, and the confiscations are a central topic. Both *Eclogue* 1 and 9 take as their chief concern the redistribution of land. The first begins with a conversation between the shepherds Meliboeus and Tityrus about the recent petition for the recovery of the estate; the ninth focuses on the disruption and loss caused by the resettlements. In an allegorical reading, Tityrus may represent Vergil, who went to Rome and appealed successfully to Octavian for the return of his farm. Perhaps from these poems it is possible to glimpse the personal loss of the poet suffered in the resettlement of soldiers.

2. The Garden of Politics

Confiscation and redistribution of land were on the minds of both Vergil and Horace at this time, although they chose to express their concerns in very different ways. One final point of contact between the satires of Horace and the *Eclogues* is made explicit in *Satire* 2.2. In this essay on the advantages of simple fare, Horace begins by characteristically occluding the poem's authority: 'This is not my *sermo*, but the words of the farmer Ofellus' (2.2.2). The advice given by the poet thus derives from a farmer who finally holds forth himself in the last twenty-one lines of the poem. Ofellus, it turns out, lived near Venusia, one of the towns marked out for booty. After describing a simple country evening with friends, food, drink, and games, Ofellus resigns himself to the state of affairs:

> Let Fortune rage and set into motion new upheavals, how much can she diminish that? By how much have you or I, boys, bloomed more sparingly since the new settler came? For Nature has settled neither that man nor me nor anyone as master of that land forever. That man drove us out; either negligence or ignorance of cunning law, or a long-lived heir will certainly drive him out in the end. Now the field is named after Umbrenus, before it was called Ofellus'. It will belong to no one, but it will pass in use, now by me, now by another. So then, live bravely, and set brave hearts against your troubles (*Satire* 2.2.126-36).

This is a rare account of a farmer's first-hand experience of land confiscation – couched as it is in the slippery genre of satire. Nevertheless, the sentiments are believable. As white bones promise that land is transformed in a cycle from ploughed field to battlefield and back again to farmland, so Ofellus trusts that the cycle of land ownership will bring his plot back to him. Osgood (2006, 212) teases out all of the implications of the 'wheel of fortune' in these lines. The veteran who drove out Ofellus will himself be driven out when the wheel turns again. This return, however, depends on legerdemain, for 'Fortune' is slyly transformed into 'Nature', and the arbitrary distribution of goods is thus equated with the natural order of the universe. Once again Horace expresses the redemptive powers of transformation.

Long after the triumvirate, Horace in the *Epistles* recounts the loss of his own family estate: 'As soon as Philippi had dismissed me from the front, humbled with clipped wings, all my father left me lost, both house and farm, audacious poverty forced me to write verses' (*Epistle* 2.2.49-52). In different genres and distinct styles, both Vergil and Horace express similar misgivings about the morality of their good fortune – and ultimately their survival – during times that brought so much distress to so many fellow citizens (cf. Mankin 1995, 64). In the end, it does not matter whether Vergil and Horace suffered personal loss – or gain – as a result of the triumviral redistribution of land. The manifestation of anxiety that their poetry expresses over loss, and gain, in the poetry – for example, *Eclogue* 1, 9, and *Satire* 2.2, to which I add *Satire* 1.8 with its Gardens of Maecenas – speaks to the widespread experience of their fellow citizens.

VI

Set aside, if you must, the possibility that this poem conveys an important message about the political circumstances under which it was produced. Yet even if I admit that it is a stretch to believe that a poem that showcases a fart so prominently could carry any political significance, there is one more avenue of inquiry that might convince you that this poem has a startling message and does indeed serve a larger purpose than sheer entertainment, mere emulation of Greek literary antecedents, simple structural filler, or the incessant reworking of Vergil, that cottage industry of Roman poets (and their modern readers). The seminal study by Richlin (first published in 1983 and revised in 1992) of sexuality and aggression in Roman humour has permanently changed the way we can read such poems as *Satire* 1.8, for by observing the prescriptive function of obscene and aggressive humour in Latin literature, she has shown that aggressive humour reinforces aggressive behaviour. Not only does Priapus' loud, obnoxious passing of gas eventually prevail over the witches, but Horace's poem about this loud, obnoxious fart continues to prevail over the delicate sensibilities of his audiences both ancient and modern. Horace gets the last laugh on the reader who blushes at his words (some compliment to Maecenas!). Invective, deriving from a sense of inadequacy or weakness, compensates for impotence (Fitzgerald 1988, 189, Oliensis 1991, 122). I argue that departure from decorum in *Satire* 1.8 not only compensates for, but ultimately inverts impotence. The inability of Priapus to do something violent to the witches leaves Horace a chance to do something permanent to his reader: to write a poem that will always, every time, put the reader in an awkward position. As Priapus is charged by his master with the task of 'scaring off thieves with penis red' (Parker 72), so Horace guards the garden of satire, driving off the sceptic who would steal from the force of his poem with words that must be read, even if denied, disregarded, or dissociated. In his transgression of generic decorum, Horace wins.

According to the statue of Priapus, the transformation of the garden from a cemetery allows for a much more pleasing stroll along a sunny embankment (*Satire* 1.8.14-15). Apparently this embankment, the remains of the Servian wall, was a well-known feature of the topography of ancient Rome. Wiseman has traced the vestiges of this time-worn rampart. From here, one might have seen (among other things) tombs, vineyards, barracks, a performing monkey or an extempore orator. Walking this *agger apricus*, one sees 'a cross-section of Roman life, luxury and poverty, beauty and squalor, love and death' (Wiseman 1998, 22). Such a promenade suits the appetites of satire, a genre of abundance and variety, composed of varied ingredients. At the end of the causeway are the Gardens of Maecenas. Suetonius relates that in the fateful year 64 CE, the emperor Nero, in full theatrical costume and singing 'The Sack of Troy', witnessed the conflagration of the city of Rome from the *turris Maecenatiana*, a tower in the gardens (*Life of Nero* 38.2). What a fitting anecdote with which to conclude. For from the tower of Maecenas in that famous garden, Nero would have been able to survey the valley between the Caelian and Oppian hills, the region he would soon transform into his most extravagant and transgressive architectural masterpiece, the *Domus Aurea*. The Julio-Claudian lust for *horti Romani* is the subject of the next chapter.

3

The Garden of Representation

It is the case with gardens as with societies: some
things require to be *fixed* so that others may be *placed*.
                                        Ian Hamilton Finlay

I

Gardens transform those who write about them and induce a trance-
like mode that abandons rational analysis and revels in the beauty
and pleasure of the moment; this disjunction in the conceptual analysis of gardens is evident in Latin literature. In his garden poem,
Columella admits that he has got carried away and that his excitement over the subject matter has caused him to stray from his strictly
didactic mode. He wakes from this temporary reverie and reminds
himself of his audience. Horace *Satire* 1.8 is a farcical piece about male
anxieties over the inability to control women. The narrator of the poem,
a statue of Priapus that resides in the Gardens of Maecenas, is carried
away by the bizarre rituals performed before his eyes; with a fart, he
comically transforms himself back to his proper function as protector of
the garden. Tacitus *Annals* 11, which includes an account of the death of
Messalina (the wife of the emperor Claudius) in the Gardens of Lucullus,
is a historical narrative that likewise addresses male anxieties over the
inability to control transgressive women. The historian also interrupts
the narrative with an assertion in the first person that betrays the
transformative powers that the garden has over his imagination.

   Although historian and poet both write about events that take place
in a garden, they respond to the garden's seduction in fundamentally
different ways that reflect the distinction between history and poetry
made by Aristotle:

   The difference between the historian and the poet is not that the
   historian employs prose and the poet verse – the work of Herodo-

65

tus could be put into verse, and it would be no less a history with verses than without them; rather the difference is that the one tells of things that have been and the other of such things as might be (*Poetics* 1451a35-b1).

This often quoted statement raises several points of contrast; for instance, the historian narrates the probable, the poet the possible. Garden narratives, however, appear to invert this principle. In poetry, the narrator (Priapus and Columella, for example) awakens from a reverie, from a dream-like trance induced by the beauty and pleasure of the garden, and returns himself to a reality, to a task at hand, to a responsibility. In the garden, the poet moves from such things as might be (Columella from the beauty of the garden, Priapus from bizarre witchcraft) and returns himself to the probable, to things as they are, to his didactic or apotropaic function. The historian, however, seems to recall himself *from* the probable. In the garden, the historian moves away from such things as they are, and resigns himself to narrating the possible so that he is able to tell the story. For the historian, representation is a refuge – like a garden; even here, however, Tacitus finds no comfort.

II

A book that tackles the theme of transgression in Latin literature is by default a book about women, and, so like Canidia in the previous chapter, Messalina holds our attention for the remainder of this chapter. The woman at the centre of *Annals* 11 is everything a Julio-Claudian woman should be, or ends up being: powerful and vulnerable; maternal and wanton; necessary and superfluous. In fact, there is little in the character of Messalina that had not been encountered in a Julio-Claudian before. To the extent that she is part Livia (wife of Augustus) by virtue of her schemes, part Julia (daughter of Augustus) by virtue of her sexual licence, part Agrippina the Elder (granddaughter of Augustus) by virtue of her maternal instincts, part Agrippina the Younger (great-granddaughter of Augustus) by virtue of her seductive powers, she represents the gradual accretion of female characteristics over four generations. Although it is impossible to escape a portrait of Messalina methodically tarred by all four of our surviving sources, at least some general assumptions about her can help us evaluate the fiction (Wyke 2002, 321-90 traces the ways this fiction permeates Messalina's *Nachleben*. For a masterful treatment of the same methodological problems in the case of Agrippina the Younger, see Ginsburg 2006).

Valeria Messalina was the great-granddaughter of Augustus' sister Octavia, and at a tender age she was married to her second cousin Claudius (who was approximately fifty years old at the time). Tacitus' portrait of her sexual exploits is monochromatic, and most likely misleading; recall that the rhetoric of women in Roman literature casts them as opposite of men. When women usurp power beyond their means, they constitute a threat that must be controlled. All sources exaggerate sexual transgression so as to control perceptions of women. It is also important to remember the fundamental disjunction between the specific portrayal of a woman like Messalina and the stereotype of the licentious empress in general. Messalina herself leaves no historical record, no memoirs, no autobiography; only the texts of male authors record her life, and these texts adhere to certain rhetorical principles which lie at the heart of historiography, biography, and satire. Finally, Messalina demonstrates the tendency of Roman gendered discourse to be engrossed with departures from the established norms. Like Canidia in *Satire* 1.8, Messalina is also an anomaly both sexually and morally, socially and even religiously, and these departures from the norm serve as symbolic frameworks for identifying and denigrating the fundamental nature of women. When such assumptions as these are kept firmly in mind, then interpretation is more likely to resist reproducing a male-centred point of view. Thus, the Messalina at the centre of Tacitus' narrative is both specific and symbolic.

In the literary records of the life of Messalina, history intersects with satire; in both, there is gendered rhetoric to disassemble. She is lampooned by Juvenal (contemporary of Tacitus) whose sexually explicit depictions create indelible impressions that permanently affect one's perception of her. In his particularly graphic sixth satire, Juvenal describes how as soon as Claudius fell asleep, Messalina would sneak out of the house in a blonde wig and make straight for the brothel where she would 'strip off, showing her gilded nipples and your womb, noble Britannicus' (Juvenal 6.122-4). She then spent the whole night in business, outlasting the prostitutes, the pimp, and even her customers.

Such invective as this reveals the deep-seated anxiety over Messalina's inherent power as a mother of potential emperors. While formal channels of direct participation in government were closed to women, informal opportunities made their indirect participation in important areas of Roman society possible. A woman could count for more than the average senator by virtue of her ability to marry and beget legitimate heirs. Women of wealthy, powerful families could exercise a degree of influence through their husbands or sons; women of the Imperial household wielded a great deal more. Indeed, the women of the *domus Augusta* had a difficult task, for they were to provide legitimate heirs to power, but not too many. It was a difficult balance to strike, not least because of the accidents of chance – that more females were born, that more males died prematurely (Corbier 1995). Nevertheless, Augustus and his successors had to depend on these women, and their benefit to a stable society outweighed whatever threat they were seen to pose. Thus, women were both beneficial and dangerous (Skinner 1997, 10-11; Parker 1998, 154-5). Juvenal's depiction of Messalina as an insatiable whore whose womb bore Britannicus articulates the anxiety this duality caused.

Of all of Messalina's outrageous acts, she was most remembered for her infamous marriage to Silius while she was still married to the emperor Claudius. This fantastic story also finds its way into Juvenal's invective: 'She sits there, waiting for him, veiled as a bride, while a marriage bed is prepared in the gardens' (10.333-5). Only this time, rather than attack her indispensable ability to produce legitimate children and so perpetuate the dynasty, Juvenal assails her inescapable omnipotence. The explicit abuse is directed at Messalina, while the implicit insult is laid upon Claudius for his impotence: '... until the affair is known throughout the city and finally reaches the ear of the emperor. He will be the last to know of his family scandal' (10.340-2). Although Messalina died in 48 CE, still both Tacitus and Juvenal found her stories irresistible decades later. The sexually explicit language of Juvenal supplements and contextualizes Tacitus' account and proves that he was not alone in his attention to the problems that Messalina symbolized, caused, and to some extent shouldered.

3. The Garden of Representation

From the outset, the most prominent problem that plagued the Julio-Claudian principate was succession. The one thing a dynasty fears most is sterility. Because Augustus never begat a son, he was never guaranteed a successor. He tried grooming members of his extended family; he favoured especially young men who might live long enough to rule successfully. But his nephew Marcellus and his grandsons Gaius and Lucius all died prematurely. He even considered some who were not members of his family as possible candidates, although they too had their problems. For instance, his confidant and second-in-command Agrippa was not of noble blood. Before he died, Augustus described three men who might rise in his place: Marcus Lepidus was capable but indifferent, Asinius Gallus was ambitious but inferior, and Lucius Arruntius was not only up to the task but he was daring as well (*Annals* 1.13.2). It appears as if Augustus tried to appoint any and every available option rather than submit to the inevitable. His step-son Tiberius (son of his second wife Livia by her first husband) was most certainly not his first choice.

Throughout the *Annals*, Tacitus foreshadows future emperors, thereby underscoring the instability of the dynasty. For example, early in the *Annals* he says of Claudius that the very last man marked out for empire by public opinion was the one whom fortune was holding in reserve as the emperor (3.18.4). The marriage of the parents of the emperor Nero is prominently placed at the end of Book 4 and is juxtaposed with the opening of Book 5 and the obituary of Livia, by whose maternal machinations Tiberius became emperor. To his account of the wedding of the soon-to-be-emperor Caligula, Tacitus appends the prophecy of Tiberius that 'You too, Galba, will some day have a taste of empire' (6.20.2). Upon his death Tiberius handed over his mask of dissimulation to Caligula (6.50). At the very moment that Nero was hailed emperor he worried where his rival Britannicus was (12.69).

Although Tacitus' account of the accession of Claudius is lost, nevertheless the account of the Jewish historian Josephus leaves no doubt about the insecurity of the transfer of the principate. When the emperor Caligula was assassinated in 41, Claudius kept to the shadows, suspecting he was in danger by virtue of his relation to Caligula. Terrified by the violence and alarmed for his own safety, he hid in an alcove. One of the city guards discovered Claudius and brought him

69

forth; the soldiers hailed him as emperor (*Jewish Antiquities* 19.1-273). That same year, Britannicus was born. The child's safety was by no means guaranteed. If Claudius were assassinated, it was not certain that Britannicus would survive and inherit the principate. Since Messalina could reasonably expect to outlive her husband, his successor would be an enemy toward her children; she had a definite interest in protecting Claudius at least until Britannicus reached maturity (Ehrhardt 1978, 56-7). Or, if Claudius were deposed, she could protect Britannicus if she were to seduce the usurper. While it may seem as though Messalina is an insatiable whore, perhaps she is just practical, hoping that, if she cannot protect her husband, at least she can protect her son. Therefore, even though her efforts proved futile, Juvenal's portrait of the nymphomaniac ought to be tempered by pragmatic considerations (Levick 1990, 56).

After ten years of marriage, whether because of sexual depravity or because of dynastic instability (and Tacitus seems to favour the former explanation), Messalina contrived to marry Gaius Silius, the consul elect for the next year (49) and a plausible replacement for the emperor by virtue of his high birth. He was the most handsome youth of the Roman nobility according to the superlatives of both Tacitus (*pulcherrimum*, 11.12.2) and Juvenal (*formosissimus*, 10.331). He divorced his wife and allowed himself to be courted by the infatuated empress. According to Tacitus, she brought him so many gifts from the imperial household that it seemed as if command of Rome had passed from Claudius to Silius. Although Silius urged her to come clean about the affair, she waited until Claudius set out for a religious festival in Ostia and then celebrated a wedding ceremony behind his back. The courtiers were appalled and informed Claudius. In fear, Messalina set out to meet Claudius on the road from Ostia, but she was prevented from an audience. She retreated to her recently acquired Gardens of Lucullus, where she waited for the executioner. She tried, upon the urging of her mother, to commit suicide but lacked the strength, both physical and moral; she was dispatched by a soldier sent to kill her.

III

This episode in Tacitus' *Annals* is central to no fewer than three studies published in the 1990s. In their contributions to *Horti Romani*,

3. The Garden of Representation

Beard and Boatwright each explore the function of literary representations of gardens in Roman culture, and both rely on *Annals* 11 to demonstrate their arguments. Beard shows that a garden is a dynamic and ambiguous space; it is not always clear who belongs in it or what constitutes proper moral behaviour in it. As Messalina craved to own the Gardens of Lucullus, so Claudius' next (and last) wife Agrippina the Younger coveted these pleasure gardens and trumped up charges against the owner. There is really no difference between the two women, and Agrippina's longing for the Gardens of Lucullus immediately spells her demise. In conclusion, Beard asserts that in the empire, gardens are a place of imperial self-fashioning, 'where the emperor could *see himself* as emperor, and so learn to be the imperial subject' (Beard 1998, 32, emphasis original). Boatwright, on the other hand, offers a more gendered reading of Roman gardens from the late Republic to the death of Nero. She argues that in the transformation from Republic to Empire, a kind of gender-bending was at work. *Horti* are emblematic of luxury, licentiousness, and most significantly, the inversion of gendered roles in political life. Gardens were depicted in historiography as the domains of either domineering women or effeminate men (Boatwright 1998). Joshel takes the Tacitean episode head on, as a symptom of the 'discourse of empire.' Messalina, with her insatiable lust, becomes merely a sign of male fears about women's power. Tacitus draws on the commonplaces of Roman moral rhetoric that associates uncontrolled female sexuality with chaos; Messalina is consistently portrayed as unconstrained and voracious. Joshel argues that Tacitus projects these undesirable attributes of Messalina onto his depiction of imperial geography and imperial power itself (Joshel 1997, 242).

Obviously I am sympathetic to the cultural and gendered approaches of these three scholars. I am also indebted to their definitions; both Beard and Boatwright are careful to distinguish between the kitchen garden of the simple Roman home, and the luxuriant pleasure Gardens (with a capital G) of the late Republic. But I would like to explore the way Tacitus narrates the death of Messalina, and how his peculiar narration is symptomatic of his historiographical method throughout the *Annals*. His inclusion and exclusion of material parallel the principles of inclusion and exclusion that define the garden. The episode also betrays a concern that the

71

representation of the events will fall short of the reality it attempts to portray. As my interpretation of *Satire* 1.8 demonstrated the potential of the Gardens of Maecenas to convey the poet's anxiety over a changing political landscape, so I argue that *Annals* 11.26-38 likewise reveals the historian's anxiety over his ability to render a credible past; for if there is one thing that the story of Messalina lacks, it is credibility.

As part of his official duties, the emperor Claudius left Rome for Ostia to perform a routine sacrifice. In his absence, his wife Messalina openly married her recently divorced lover Silius. Even in social circles steeped in widespread adultery, such reckless disregard for marriage was unprecedented. Just as soon as Tacitus embarks on narrating this travesty, he spends an entire paragraph relating the details of the wedding in a disclaimer for the story he is about to tell:

> I am scarcely unaware that it will seem to be a remarkable story that any mortal had such a sense of security in a city which is aware of everything and silent about nothing, that a consul-elect with the wife of the emperor on an appointed day, with witnesses to certify, should have come together as if for the sake of rearing children, that she should have listened to the omens, taken vows, and performed sacrifices to the gods, reclined among guests, giving kisses and embraces and finally spending the night in the licence of the married. But I relate nothing out of sensationalism (*miraculi causa*), but what was heard and written by my elders (11.27).

In this statement of authorial self-assertion, Tacitus collides head-on with the disparity in the conceptual analysis of gardens in a distinctly historical way. The intrusion of the first person into the narrative can be compared to the first person assertion of Columella half way through his garden poem, or to the wood-splitting fart at the end of *Satire* 1.8 that reminds the reader of Priapus' status as wooden object. Likewise, Tacitus calls attention to the status of his history as written document, and his status as author; however, he places this assertion at the *beginning* of his account. Rather than recall himself from a garden reverie, here he seems to steel himself against the powers of the garden to lead a rational reader astray. Aware of the possibility for seduction, Tacitus defuses the power of the garden at the outset.

72

3. The Garden of Representation

By embedding the juicy details (the appointed day, witnesses, sacrifices, banquet, and finally even the consummation) in an open admission of disbelief, Tacitus disarms the story. Such a self-proclaimed loss for words, 'I am scarcely unaware that it will seem to be a remarkable story,' lends a degree of innocence to the narrative. It also serves to inoculate the statements that follow. By admitting that the story is far-fetched, Tacitus actually asserts rhetorical control over the intractable material. He immunizes the less than trustworthy contents of the ensuing narrative from a debilitating loss of credibility by means of a small injection of openly acknowledged disbelief (cf. Barthes 1972, 150-1). Thus Tacitus both exculpates himself and mitigates the effect of what follows. Such self-proclaimed statements of disbelief may also serve another concurrent function in the narrative. An admission that, 'I am scarcely unaware that it will seem to be a remarkable story,' establishes the reader's confidence that he is in the hands of a sensible narrator, one who is prepared to admit the strangeness of his material. The historian is most trustworthy at precisely those moments when he openly denies his naïveté.

With little else but his own common sense to verify the story, Tacitus must report what he has at his disposal. He displaces the responsibility for the veracity of the story onto his 'elders' and thereby occludes his own role in the formulation of the account (Meise 1969, 123-7; Mehl 1974, 90-5). Tacitus exonerates himself with an appeal to common sense when he denies a taste for the scandalous: 'I relate nothing out of sensationalism.' Tacitus assumes an air of superiority over his sources that merely gives the impression of advancing historical understanding beyond the sordid details that in fact form the substance of the paragraph.

The imperial court hastily responded to the outrageous wedding; everyone was aghast. All agreed that under no circumstances should Claudius grant an audience to his errant wife, even to hear her confession (11.28). Claudius' three closest advisors (all imperial freedmen), Pallas, Callistus, and Narcissus, debated the best way to handle the situation. Pallas was too much of a coward to get involved, Callistus too wise. Only Narcissus took it upon himself to inform Claudius of the illegal wedding (11.29). The calculating imperial freedman did not tell Claudius himself but enlisted two of the emperor's regular prostitutes to reveal the marriage. Calpurnia told Claudius that Mes-

salina married Silius; Cleopatra corroborated the story. Their fortui-
tous names allow Tacitus to hint at the homonymous wife (Calpurnia)
and mistress (Cleopatra) of Julius Caesar and the conspiracy to assassinate the dictator that was no doubt deeply embedded in Roman
collective memory. Indeed, Tacitus often plays upon the etymological
meanings of names for various effect (Sinclair 1995, 30-1; Woodman
and Martin 1996, 491-3; Woodman 1998, 221-2; Ash 1999, 59).

Attention to names lets us apprehend a possible allusion in the
name of the freedman. Narcissus is the name of a flower, suitable
enough in a narrative that leads to a garden. According to classical
mythology, Narcissus was a young man cursed to love himself and
never attain the object of his affection. Quenching his thirst beside a
pool of water, Narcissus sees his own reflection and falls in love. He
tries in vain to kiss and embrace but the reflection eludes his grasp:
'Foolish boy, why do you seek in vain these fleeting images? What you
seek is nowhere: should you turn away, you would destroy that which
you love. That which you see is a shadow of a reflected form and has
no substance of its own' (Ovid, *Metamorphoses* 3.432-5). At the heart
of the story of Narcissus is the paradox of representation. Insubstan-
tial images are deceptive and can lead to disappointment and even
despair. It is worth keeping this moral lesson in mind as we read about
the destruction of Messalina. Just as Narcissus cannot attain the
object of his desire, so the historian has difficulty apprehending his
subject matter. History, itself a representation of the past, can slip
through the fingers as easily as a reflection in a pool of water. Together
with Tacitus' disclaimer of veracity in *Annals* 11.27, the association of
Narcissus' name with the deceptive power of representation is, I
believe, another clue to the anxiety of representation that suffuses
Tacitus' account of the fall of Messalina.

Upon learning of the marriage ceremony, Claudius consulted his
most powerful friends, all of whom confirmed the story. Meanwhile,
Messalina and Silius celebrated a masquerade of the sacred rites of
the vintage:

But Messalina, more unbridled in her luxury than ever, as
autumn approached, celebrated a masquerade of a vintage festival at home. Presses were trodden, vats were flowing, and women
girt with wild beast skins were dancing about like bacchantes

performing sacrifices or rapt with frenzy. She let her hair down and was shaking a thyrsus; nearby Silius encircled with ivy was wearing the tragic costume, tossing his head, with a brash chorus clamouring about (11.31.2).

Bacchic revelry is the hallmark of female misconduct, and here Tacitus calls upon a vast tradition of maenad behaviour in Greek and Latin art and literature, where women are seen to toss back their heads and expose their necks, roll their eyes, howl like beasts, foam at the mouth, trample the ground, stampede through woods, and finally turn into savage beasts themselves, killing domestic animals and devouring raw flesh (Henrichs 1978, 122). Recall that in *Satire* 1.8, Canidia and Sagana ripped apart the flesh of a dark lamb with their (albeit false) teeth. As the Senate's extreme reaction to the Bacchanalian conspiracy of 186 BCE attests, bacchic worship touched a nerve and frightened the Romans, particularly because it ignored the traditional boundaries of status and gender. Noble or common, male or female; anyone could worship Bacchus. As we shall see, such indiscrimination in status and gender was a fundamental principle of the revolutionary Christianity that Augustine eventually embraced. By behaving as a bacchante, Messalina transgresses established expectations for a woman of her class and further degrades her social status.

Given the degree of detail lavished on this scene, it is especially curious that Tacitus refers to the event as a masquerade, a *simulacrum*, a word that hints at the historian's anxiety of representation. The entire story is so far-fetched that Tacitus calls the vintage celebration a likeness of a real festival. Tacitus' ability to represent events, no matter how skilful, eventually fails, leaving but a mere *simulacrum*. Credibility yields to verisimilitude.

The exact location of the vintage festival is not specified. The temporal setting is also vaguely described; 'as autumn approached' is the only clue. Furthermore, it is not stated precisely how much time passed since the wedding scene and whether the masquerade of the vintage festival is somehow connected with the marriage rites. Colin attempts to reconstruct the temporal sequence of events: Claudius had already gone to Ostia to officiate at the festival of the Volcanalia celebrated on 23 August; Messalina's vintage festival was celebrated on 19 August. Already by Varro's time the festival had fallen out of practice and was scarcely celebrated even among vegetable gardeners (Colin 1956, 32-3). The marriage which took place in Claudius' absence must have occurred before 19 August; Claudius was recalled to the city before he could discharge his duties in Ostia on 23 August. None of this, however, is specified in the text of Tacitus. Instead of details, Tacitus suspends a vision of the bacchantes before our eyes and fills our ears with their frenzied cries. Silius assumes buckskins and ivy, the costume of Bacchus; perhaps Messalina with her flowing hair represents Ariadne. Tacitus does not make clear for us the temporal and spatial details of the event, only its imagery, and thereby its lack of substance.

During the festivities, Vettius Valens climbed a tree and caught sight of the approaching Claudius, and 'he told those who asked him what he saw that a terrible storm was approaching from Ostia, whether such a spectacle had in fact begun or perhaps a slip of the tongue turned into a prophecy' (11.31.3). The phrase 'whether such a spectacle had in fact begun' (*siue coeperat ea species*) is quite unusual in both its diction and its syntax. Here again, Tacitus falters at the brink of explanation. The terrible storm may have been no more than a *species*, a spectacle. *Species* can also mean 'appearance', and like *simulacrum* it alerts the reader to the potential shortcomings of representation.

Claudius' approach is compared to the weather, described as merely the appearance, *species*, of a blustering storm. In this way the emperor's foolishness is further accentuated. Perhaps the comparison of Claudius' impending anger to a storm is some sort of joke on the emperor's alleged flatulence. After all, Suetonius tells how Claudius contemplated an edict allowing farting at table (*Life of Claudius* 32). Seneca the Younger immortalized Claudius' flatulence in the satirical *Apocolocyntosis*; as he died, Claudius let out a loud fart (*Apocolocyntosis* 4.3). Such portrayals of Claudius' bodily distortion, ugliness, and failure to control his bodily emissions, all attributes of sterility (Miller 1998), allow the Roman writers to condemn Claudius and his reign as ethically and politically flawed (see Braund and James 1998). The repeated references in the sources to Claudius' physical attributes, his stammers, ticks, and lopsided gait, combine to form an image of incompetence (Leon 1948; Vessey 1971; Dickison 1977; Martin 1981, 144-5, 160-1; Griffin 1990, 483; Levick 1990, 193; Mellor 1993, 25). As

Claudius is portrayed here as giving off only an appearance (*species*), so we become aware of Tacitus' incapacity to represent events clearly, in this case, to explain Vettius' cryptic remark. Tacitus exploits not the historian's probability but the poet's possibility of narrative to its fullest. He does not specify precisely at whose home or in whose garden the vintage festival took place; he does not specify when. He does not say exactly what Vettius saw but encrypts his vision in a prophecy. What matters is not the probability of the events, but the possibility of narrating them. The events may not be credible, but at least they are narrated.

Meanwhile as Claudius returns from Ostia, outside the city, Messalina retreats to the Gardens of Lucullus on the edge of the city to escape the gathering storm, while Silius alone heads straight for the Forum, the heart of Rome (11.32.1). The refuges which Messalina and Silius seek are laden with irony, and suitably so. He flees to the Forum, literally 'the place outside', an open space located in the centre of the city that was the heart of Republican political life. She chooses the gardens, an enclosed space located on the periphery of the city that symbolize a retreat from Republican ideals to imperial decadence. As violently as they were attracted to each other, so in the impending doom are they repelled as if by centrifugal force.

Yet Messalina does not rest in the garden; here she gathers her forces around her and determines to meet Claudius face to face. 'And so meanwhile with a total of three companions (so suddenly did such solitude descend) having covered the extent of the city on foot, she then set out on the Via Ostiensis on a cart which they use to carry refuse from the gardens, with no pity from anyone because the turpitude of her crimes was so manifest' (11.32.3). The catchy phrase 'the extent of the city' (*spatium urbis*) engages the time-worn cliché of 'city and world' immortalized by Ovid: 'For other nations their land is given a fixed boundary; the extent of the city of Rome is likewise the extent of the Roman world' (*spatium est urbis et orbis idem, Fasti* 2.683-4; see Bréguet 1969). Messalina's hyperbolic journey is capped with the unseemly image of the empress sitting atop a lowly cart, whose use to remove unwanted matter from the garden implies the woman is likewise unwanted (Beard 1998, 28). Besides the boldness of the comparison, however, it is one of the shining moments in the *Annals* when Tacitus breaches the limits of decorum. The cart gently reminds us that behind every flower bed is a sweaty gardener with dirt under his nails. The splendour of the dissembling garden is stripped away to reveal the terms of its materiality.

Messalina attempts to meet the returning Claudius on the Via Ostiensis and insists that her husband listen to the mother of his children (11.34). But motherhood gains her no forgiveness. Tacitus emphasizes the complete control that the freedmen and imperial courtiers hold over the situation; Claudius is isolated and immobilized. When at last he addresses the soldiers assembled in the camp in Rome to assure them that he is still in power, his words are dictated by Narcissus (11.35). The soldiers confirm their support of the emperor and demand the names of the culprits and their punishment. In addition to Silius, several others were brought forward and condemned. At last, Tacitus casts the danger imposed by the far-fetched marriage of Messalina and Silius as a potential coup d'état.

Once potential conspirators were punished, only the death of Messalina remained. In *Satire* 1.8, a cemetery was transformed into a garden. In *Annals* 11, the Gardens of Lucullus become a place for death:

> Euodus, one of the freedmen, was chosen as overseer and supervisor of the deed. Speedily having gone ahead into the gardens he found her [Messalina] poured out on the ground, with her mother Lepida sitting nearby, (who, scarcely in agreement with her daughter when she was prosperous, was overcome to pity by her final distress), and urging her not to wait for the murderer. Her life was over and she ought not seek anything else than honour in death. But since her mind was corrupted by licentiousness, nothing decent occurred to her. She kept prolonging the tears and complaints in vain, when the gates were crashed by the force of those entering. The tribune stood over her in silence, but the freedman stood over her rebuking with many lowly invectives (11.37.3).

Indifference to honourable undertakings seems to be an attribute of the sexually promiscuous woman, for Tacitus describes a low-born courtesan in similar terms. Epicharis, the heroine of the conspiracy to assassinate Nero, endures torture and death instead of betraying her fellow conspirators. Tacitus has no explanation for the bravery of this woman who did not 'have any care for decent matters before' (15.51); however, by remaining loyal to the conspiracy, Epicharis earns Tacitus' respect. He chastises the cowardly Pisonian conspirators for letting a woman, and one of such low social standing, humiliate them. By casting both Epicharis and Messalina as women who do not 'have a care for any decent matter', he emphasizes the extent to which each woman thwarted expectations of her status. A woman of Messalina's social standing was supposed to care about decency, but she did not. On the other hand, very little was expected of a woman like Epicharis, who in the end died more nobly than the empress.

If I try to reduce this passage to a single image, I am the more impressed with how Tacitus manipulates elegiac diction and Stoic allusion to create a composite historical portrait which is neither elegiac nor Stoic. The tears, complaints, and beaten doors are the hallmarks of Latin love elegy (Copley 1956, 28-42). Often an excluded lover, suffering a great indignity, sings a plaintive song to the closed door of his lover's house begging for admission. Sometimes when rebuffed, the excluded lover foolishly speculates as to whether his beloved is sleeping with another. Like the mythological figure of Narcissus, kept from his own reflection, so the excluded lover is barred from the object of his affection. Nevertheless the gates of the Gardens of Lucullus are not serenaded by an excluded lover. Instead of hearing the tears and sighs of an excluded lover through a tightly closed door, Messalina must endure the vicious taunts of a freedman to her face. Unlike the elegiac door that never opens, Messalina's garden gates succumb to the violent attack. Euodus – whose Greek name denotes 'easy access' – and the others enter her garden.

Long ago, the archaic Greek iambic poet Archilochus used the verdant softness of the garden as a metaphor for female genitalia: 'I will hold myself back in your grassy garden' (see Osborne 1992, 388). In the past, Messalina was all too ready to open her 'garden gate.' Tacitus exaggerates her affairs with the rhetorical plural: she had slept with Titiuses, Vettiuses and Plautiuses (11.30). Euodus, however, must force his entry. He does not remain an excluded lover; rather, all the indignity that an excluded lover suffers is displaced onto Messalina. Without delving into the problems of the origin of iamb, we can say with confidence that one prominent feature of the genre is the invective deployed against women. Horace invents a fictitious Canidia as the target of his invective (with Greek antecedents, to be sure; see Newman 1998; Harrison 2001). For Tacitus, on the other hand, history provides a ready target in the person of Messalina.

Elegy has one purpose: to persuade and conquer the woman; however, the poet categorically fails. This sense of victor and vanquished proffers the poets metaphors of war; the poet is forever a soldier on the battlefield of love. Tacitus' elegiac depiction of the death of Messalina takes this imagery to its extreme. The silent military tribune conquers – kills – the woman: 'in terror she was applying the sword ineffectually to her throat or breast, when the tribune drove it through her with one blow' (11.38). The penetration of the sword suggests one last sexual penetration. Where the elegiac poet fails, the military tribune succeeds. Finally, Valeria Messalina belongs to the illustrious family of Messallae, whose roots extend deep into the Republic. Perhaps for Tacitus her name evokes the name of her ancestor, Marcus Valerius Messalla Corvinus, the patron of the elegiac poet Tibullus and the soldier who figures so prominently in Tibullus' elegies. In the account of the death of Messalina, Tacitus subverts every expectation that his elegiac diction raises.

Nor is this a Stoic garden (indeed, as we shall see, if the Gardens of Lucullus have any philosophical inclination, it is Epicurean, and not Stoic), a place for education and the pruning and correction of misconceptions and the cultivation of moral rectitude. Like the plants that must be pruned of their excess growth in order to flourish, so the moral excesses of hubris and arrogance are checked in the philosopher's garden. One of the most memorable characters of the Tacitean corpus meets his death in a garden, and it is worth taking a moment to consider the life and death of the Stoic Thrasea Paetus and the contrasts between his death and the death of Messalina in the Gardens of Lucullus.

Thrasea Paetus was of consular rank and enjoyed a distinguished public career under the emperors Claudius and Nero. After Nero murdered his mother Agrippina the Younger, however, Thrasea could no longer conceal his disgust for the emperor. His withdrawal from public life was seen as an insult to the imperial court. Thrasea wrote a controversial biography of the staunchly Republican statesman Cato (enemy of Julius Caesar and so *persona non grata* among Julio-Claudian emperors). In addition, Thrasea was known to have celebrated the birthdays of Brutus and Cassius, assassins of Julius Caesar and so-called Liberators. In 66 CE, Thrasea was prosecuted and condemned for treason (a nebulous category of prosecution) by the greedy informants Cossutianus Capito and Eprius Marcellus; he committed suicide in his garden. His son-in-law Helvidius Priscus was exiled at this time, and when he returned to Rome under the emperor Galba in December 68, he carried on Thrasea's vendetta against Eprius Marcellus. Helvidius' tactless, intransigent, and flaunted independence of opinion finally earned him banishment and execution in 74.

Both Thrasea and Helvidius were the subject of encomiastic biographies that were subsequently censored. The authors Junius Rusticus and Herennius Senecio paid a high price for their writings, and the fate of these four men – two statesmen condemned to death and their biographers – haunted Tacitus throughout his literary career. Tacitus begins the *Agricola* (his father-in-law's biography of sorts, written long before the *Annals*) by recalling the condemnation of the works of Rusticus and Senecio and ends his last literary endeavour, the *Annals* (as we have it) with the death of Thrasea and exile of Helvidius. Rusticus and Senecio prove that it is difficult to praise a good man and survive.

Thrasea committed suicide in his garden; he was unjustly convicted, and yet he carried out his own death with courage and Stoic resolve. Messalina, on the other hand, could hardly commit suicide in the Gardens of Lucullus; she was patently guilty and died without any dignity whatsoever. Besides these radical differences, however, Thrasea and Messalina share one compelling similarity. Both are figures of failure and futility, and Tacitus disapproves of both. As Messalina's attempts to secure the position of her son fail, likewise Thrasea's suicide achieves no lasting results. A perilous career such as Thrasea's, utterly useless to the state and culminating in an ostentatious death, is foolhardy and scarcely recommended (*Agricola* 42.4). Unlike the biographer Rusticus, who paid a price for his account of the death of Thrasea, Tacitus pays no penalty for his account of the death of Messalina. The scope for writing about good men is narrow, and treacherous; however, there is always plenty of room to write about evil women.

81

Unlike the starvation of Cremutius Cordus or Drusus (4.35.4, 6.23.2), where a bloodless death is decorously left off the page, unlike the staged suicides of Seneca the Younger, Lucan, or Petronius (15.63, 15.70, 16.19), where the victim chooses for himself what is likely to be the less violent alternative, the death of Messalina is forcefully put before the reader's eye. She kept trying in vain to kill herself with a dagger until a blow from the soldier drove it through her. In the Gardens of Lucullus, like a flower (*florenti*, 11.37.3) poured upon the earth (*fusam humi*, 11.37.3) in the prime of her, life she is felled. Nor is Messalina granted famous last words, like Claudius' next – and last – wife Agrippina the Younger, another imperial woman fated to a violent death (her last words were 'Strike my womb', 14.8.5). Her body was handed over to her mother – yet another woman rendered sterile by the death of the only child that could produce a possible heir to the throne. Although Lepida was inextricably entangled in the root system of the Julio-Claudian family tree (she was the daughter of the younger Antonia, grand-niece of Augustus, cousin of Agrippina the Younger, and aunt of Nero), nevertheless none of these relationships could save her or her daughter from destruction.

To sum up my observations: Tacitus begins his account of the death of Messalina with an over-determined disclaimer that bespeaks his anxiety over his ability to represent events credibly. The freedman who takes charge of the situation has the provocative name of Narcissus, calling to mind the fragility of representation and the frustration of obtaining the object of desire. The vintage festival is referred to as a masquerade (*simulacrum*); Claudius' return to Rome is seen as a spectacle (*species*). The death scene in the garden is composed of elegiac diction, but it is not elegiac. It foreshadows the Stoic death of Thrasea, but it is not philosophically paradigmatic. Furthermore, time is both compacted and expanded. The mention of the *horti Luculliani* at the beginnings of 11.32 and 11.37 forms a ring-composition which robs us of the sense of time which the accusations, trials, and executions of the 'conspirators' would require. Such repetition negates the forward temporal progress of the narrative. Space is exaggerated or altogether ignored; Messalina is said to have travelled the extent of the city in the cart, a distance that with an Ovidian slip of the tongue, can sound as if she travelled the extent of the world. On the other hand, the distance between the place of the bacchic revelry and the Via

Ostiensis does not matter to Vettius' drunken prophecy; he can see quite far from his perch atop the tree. The whole episode defies temporal and spatial precision. Given that gardens are inherently rooted in time and space, the imprecision is especially striking and reveals once again the disjunction in the conceptual analysis of gardens.

IV

Behind Messalina, Claudius, Narcissus, behind the sexual indiscretion and the grisly murder, behind all that transpires in *Annals* 11 looms the figure of the able Republican general Lucius Licinius Lucullus, original owner of the garden. It would be very easy to identify Lucullus with greed, avarice, luxury, and extravagance. For instance, to construct his villa in Campania, he defied nature and built out over the sea and dug into mountainsides. Stories about his luxurious dining habits are ubiquitous. His dining room was equipped with an aviary; his guests drank from cups thickly encrusted with jewels; he punished a slave who brought him a modest meal although he was dining alone. Lucullus is easily a symbol of excessive, decadent living; however, there is more to the man than the stories of his late biographer Plutarch, who relied on an already well established negative literary heritage that systematically blackened Lucullus' character. Attention to his whole career adds another dimension to his gardens in Rome as an especially meaningful setting for the demise of Messalina.

Lucullus began his career under Sulla as a military tribune in the Social Wars. From 88 to 80 BCE he served as a treasurer in the east; thus he was in Asia during the dreaded proscriptions of Sulla and avoided participation in the man-hunts and slaughter. He was elected consul in 74; after his consulship, he was given command of forces in the east, where he spent all of his efforts attempting to subdue Mithridates, king of Pontus. When reading *Annals* 11, the reader is struck by the predominance of material on Parthia and Armenia. Keitel argues that Tacitus creates a 'contrapuntal' effect between events at Rome and those in the East; dynastic intrigue and instability threatens both Parthia and Rome (Keitel 1978). Such prolonged accounts of Parthia and Armenia in *Annals* 11, however, also cause the reader to reflect on the long standing enmity between Rome and Parthia. Lucullus was one of the earliest leading players in that conflict.

The ancient state of Armenia was located between the two powerful empires of Rome and Parthia. The hope of conquering Armenia and increasing its status in the Empire from a client-kingdom to a province continually tempted Roman generals. Having achieved success against Mithridates, Lucullus carried the war into Armenia in 69 BCE and occupied the city of Tigranocerta, which he so thoroughly dismantled that it was never to be an important city again. He continued toward the capital city of Artaxata but his effort ultimately failed because of hesitation, mismanagement, and insubordination. By 67, Lucullus' political enemies in Rome insisted that he step down; he had held command long enough. In 66, the Senate passed the *Lex Manilia*, handing over all military command to Pompey. Lucullus was unceremoniously relieved of his duty and returned to Rome.

Because of the political opposition that favoured Pompey, Lucullus had to wait three years before he could hold his triumphal procession. In 59 BCE he attempted to stop the ratification of Pompey's eastern arrangements and veteran settlements; his failure to do so only brought him disgrace. At this point, he appears to have recognized the limits of his power and position and to have created a life that pursued private pleasure (Keaveney 1992, 156). Always an Epicurean, he spent the rest of his life in refined luxury. He began construction on his famous gardens on the Pincian Hill, where other great statesmen of the Republic, including Pompey and Messalla Corvinus, also built gardens. The Gardens of Lucullus were bounded on the west by the Via di Porta Pinciana and extended to the top of the hill (Kaster 1974, 14-15; Broise and Jolivet 1985, 749; Grimal 1984, 128 and 272 fig. 32). These were refurbished some eighty years later by Valerius Asiaticus in 47 CE; the renovations caused Messalina to lust after the gardens and to contrive the ruin of Asiaticus, upon whose death she acquired the property. Built by a figure of futility, the Gardens of Lucullus embody the escapism and extravagance of the wealthy in the face of a declining Republic. The exigencies of political life forced Lucullus to lay down his *negotium* for a world of *otium*. As the Gardens of Maecenas signify a changing landscape, the Gardens of Lucullus suggest a changing morality.

Tacitus does not dwell on Lucullus' reputation for extravagant living; rather, his moral weakness is implied. Lucullus is mentioned five times in the *Annals* in his capacity as general of the east, and three of these times he is named together with Pompey (*Annals* 12.62, 13.34, 15.14). To a certain extent, therefore, Tacitus openly affords Lucullus his reputation as an able general. As Tacitus underscores Roman failure to gain Armenia, he thereby points to Lucullus' part in the attempt, and failure, of empire. The creator of the Gardens of Lucullus was a general who was unable to accomplish anything substantial, who was followed by a series of generals as great, or greater than he, who also failed to subdue Parthia. What Lucullus did leave behind to posterity, however, were two significant estates, both of which Tacitus exploits for his moral message. Tiberius died in Lucullus' villa in Campania; Messalina in the Gardens of Lucullus in Rome. Lucullus' permanent contribution to Rome was to provide suitable settings for the deaths of degenerate nobles. Both villa and garden are monuments to futility; they represent a permanent retreat that in the end lasted longer than any military achievement. The ineffective Lucullus and the unsuccessful Messalina are outcasts in the luxurious pleasure garden on the fringes of the bustle of Rome.

V

From the way Tacitus handles the death of Messalina, we can apprehend something of his philosophy of history writing. Because we are now attuned to the anxiety of representation in this episode, we can see how Tacitus' statements of method scattered throughout the *Annals* further articulate this anxiety.

In the account of Messalina's death, Tacitus struggles to depict material that proves intractable at nearly every turn. In the use of the words *simulacrum* and *species* (synonyms meaning 'image' or 'representation'), Tacitus struggles with a moral issue: how to shape a narrative that most closely approximates but can never virtually reproduce the past. The paradox of history is that it is inseparable from the rhetoric that gives it shape. All Tacitus can do is write the *Annals*; the rest – the past which he records and the future to which he leaves his record – is beyond his control. Hence he uses the hortatory subjunctive (instead of a definite indicative): '*Let this be granted* to the posterity of illustrious men ...' (*Annals* 16.16.2). If he does not succeed in providing the most realistic representation, if he does not satisfy the expectations that Republican history raises (for example, accounts of huge wars, sacked cities, kings routed and cap-tured, as listed at *Annals* 4.32), nevertheless he does succeed in providing some degree of moral instruction, even if by negative exam-ple: 'For this I believe to be history's highest function, that virtues be not silenced and that fear of disgrace from posterity should attend crooked words and deeds' (*Annals* 3.65.1). Most of all, he succeeds in materializing, however fleetingly, the anxiety of all those who live with the knowledge that their lives and their appearance fail dismally in comparison to the past and to reality.

One could say every author dissimulates, every author disguises his aporia, transgresses the parameters of his work, fears that he will be misunderstood. That we can detect the aporia ought to prove that the work is inferior; a good text disguises its incapacities. To be sure, Tacitus is successful at representing the Julio-Claudian dynasty. In-deed, Tacitus overcomes the difficulties and leaves a legible record. By recognizing the anxiety of representation in the *Annals*, however, we can appreciate the magnitude of Tacitus' achievement. In order to narrate the recent past safely, he must perform a balancing act, the results of which barely compensate for the inherent dangers:

> The descendants of many who suffered hardship or shame under Tiberius still remain, and even if the families themselves have now died out, still you will find those who think the sins of others are cast in their faces because they resemble their own behav-iour. Even praise and virtue have their enemies, as exposing their opposites from too close a position (4.33.4).

If Tacitus is this worried about his ability to write of the reign of Tiberius safely, then he must also have grave reservations about his ability to write of the even more recent reign of Claudius. But he does, and he survives. Unlike Rusticus and Senecio who praise their sub-jects outright, Tacitus engages in a very different brand of encomium. By showing the Julio-Claudians in as unfavourable light as he can, he casts a favourable light on his current emperor in inverse proportion. For Tacitus, praise is not that which is articulated but that which is left unspoken. Thus, he concludes the prologue of the biography of his father in law Agricola – the man who, above all others demonstrated that it *is* possible to be a good man under a bad emperor – by saying 'we should have lost memory as well as voice, had it been as easy to forget as to keep silence' (*Agricola* 2). Silence is easy; forgetting is the hard part.

Perhaps Tacitus tried to escape the dangers of politics in the leisure of history, but there too he found only anxiety (cf. Syme 1970, 11-12). In the *Annals* he describes a world where emperors fear freedom and hate slavery (2.87); he advocates that the only hope is to steer a moderate course between the two. Even so, only a few naturally talented men – and Agricola comes to mind immediately – are capable of this. Under such circumstances one cannot afford to be outspoken; nor does silence offer any assurances (4.60.2). For the historian, as for the statesmen he writes about, silence is always an easy option; not the most noble but surely the most salubrious (for an interpretation of the etymology of the name Tacitus meaning 'silence', see Hedrick 2000).

The historian with his expertise knows how to tend his *Annals*, how to hold his peace. In the garden of history, like the garden of satire, the continued presence of the rejected other points to a logic of exclusion at the heart of the act of gardening, and by extension writing about gardens and gardening: exclusion is always ultimately self-un-dermining and unsustainable. There must always be something or someone to eject; the achievement of purity destroys the boundaries that define it, thereby destroying any ability to discern difference. Neither *Satire* 1.8 nor *Annals* 11 would exist without the transgres-sive, excluded others who insist on inhabiting the Gardens of Maecenas and Lucullus: so says Ian Hamilton Finlay, 'it is the case with gardens as with societies'. Without weeds to pull or fences to stake, the garden ceases to exist.

VI

At the beginning of this chapter, I tried to draw a distinction between the ways ancient Latin poetry and history respond to the garden's seduction and the way these genres conform to Aristotle's prescriptive definition. In Forché's 'The Garden Shukkei-en', a poem about the bomb-ing of Hiroshima in August 1945, history and poetry are inextricably intertwined and the poet-narrator experiences the transformative powers of the garden. In the restored Japanese garden Shukkei-en, history meets poetry in a haunting encounter that demonstrates once again the powerful force of gardens on the literary imagination – and the political landscape.

Shukkei-en, located in Hiroshima, is a water garden designed by Soko Ueda, a famous master of ceremonial tea, and built by the feudal lord Asano Nagaakira beginning in 1620. At the centre of Shukkei-en is Takuei pond, containing more than ten islets. Around the pond, a path connects bridges, tea cottages, and arbours. Such circular-tour gardens first appeared in the seventeenth century, in the early Edo Era (1600-1867) and were the preferred garden form of feudal lords. The wide variety of views gives the impression that Shukkei-en is much larger than it actually is. The garden is notable for its bridges; two slightly arching bridges, one monolithic and the other earthen, meet on one of the small islands where a stone lantern is constructed of rocks. The middle portion of a stone bridge is reminiscent of the arching bridge in the garden Koraku-en in Tokyo. In fact, the name 'shukkei-en' or 'shrink scenery garden' expresses the idea of collecting and miniaturizing scenic views. According to tradition, Shukkei-en in Hiroshima was built to resemble the grand gardens of Xi Hu in China.

Xi Hu, or West Lake, is a 1,235 acre lake located in Hangzhou, south of Shanghai on the sea, surrounded by many different types of structures, including a park, hotel, temple, and government guest houses (Valder 2002, 306-9). According to traditional Chinese practice, views around the lake were given descriptive names, for example, 'Melting Snow on Broken Bridge', or 'Autumn Moon on Calm Lake' (Valder 2002, 306). Visitors to the garden take a circular walking tour of the ten prospects. In the middle of the lake is a clover-leaf shaped island, on which there is a garden – with a miniature lake. Thus, West Lake itself contains a garden within a garden, a lake within a lake. At a mere 13 acres, the miniature Japanese reproduction of Shukkei-en introduces yet another layer to the embedded representations of West Lake.

In 1940, Shukkei-en was donated to the Hiroshima Prefecture and designated a national scenic spot. Its vegetation and buildings were severely damaged by fire in the atomic bombing of August 1945. Six years later, the garden was opened to the public in 1951, while restoration was still in progress. Buildings continued to be replaced in 1964 and 1974. The Hiroshima Prefectural Board of Education instituted repairs to restore its scenery and planted more than 5,000 trees and plants; today it is a popular tourist attraction to some 300,000 visitors annually. The Shukkei-en that one sees today is a restoration of a reproduction of West Lake, itself a garden that encapsulates a garden. No wonder Shukkei-en captured the imagination of the poet and political activist Forché, in her poem, 'The Garden Shukkei-en' (1994, 70-71):

> By way of a vanished bridge we cross this river
> as a cloud of lifted snow would ascend a mountain.
>
> She has always been afraid to come here.
>
> It is the river she most
> remembers, the living
> and the dead both crying for help.
>
> A world that allowed neither tears nor lamentation.
>
> The *matsu* trees brush her hair as she passes
> beneath them, as do the shining strands of barbed wire.
>
> Where this lake is, there was a lake,
> where these black pine grow, there grew black pine.
>
> Where there is no teahouse I see a wooden teahouse
> and the corpses of those who slept in it.
>
> On the opposite bank of the Ota, a weeping willow
> etches its memory of their faces into the water.
>
> Where light touches the face, the character for heart is written.
>
> She strokes a burnt trunk wrapped in straw:
> I was weak and my skin hung from my fingertips like cloth
>
> Do you think for a moment we were human beings to them?
>
> She comes to the stone angel holding paper cranes.

89

Not an angel, but a woman where she once had been,
who walks through the garden Shukkei-en
calling the carp to the surface by clapping her hands.

Do Americans think of us?

So she began as we squatted over the toilets:
If you want, I'll tell you, but nothing I say will be enough.

We tried to dress our burns with vegetable oil.

Her hair is the white froth of rice rising up kettlesides, her mind
    also.
In the postwar years she thought deeply about how to live.

The common greeting *dozo-yiroshku* is please take care of me.
All *hibakusha* still alive were children then.

A cemetery seen from the air is a child's city.

I don't like this particular flower because
it reminds me of a woman's brain crushed under a roof.

Perhaps my language is too precise, and therefore difficult to
    understand?

We have not, all these years, felt what you call happiness.
But at times, with good fortune, we experience something close.
As our life resembles life, and this garden the garden.
And in the silence surrounding us what happened to us

    it is the bell to awaken God that we've heard ringing.

In 'The Garden Shukkei-en,' the narrator and a survivor of the atom
bomb attack of 1945 stroll together through the garden in Hiroshima.
As they cross the bridge into the garden, the narrator remarks, 'She
has always been afraid to come here.' The first nine lines of the poem
recount their entrance to the garden in the third person. Then, in a

90

move that evinces the disjuncture between 'then' and 'now' (so characteristic of garden literature), the voice shifts as the survivor describes
what she sees presently in terms of what she saw that day in 1945:
'Where this lake is, there was a lake, / where these black pines grow,
there grew black pine. / Where there is no teahouse I see a wooden
teahouse / and the corpses of those who slept in it.' The survivor's
description telescopes the phenomenon of shukkei, of reproduction.
What was intended to be an aesthetic effect has in fact become a cruel
reality. The playfulness of the Japanese artistic reproduction of the
Chinese West Lake has been replaced by the barbarity of the restoration after the American attack. The reconstitution of one imperial
domination (Chinese) has been replaced by another (American), and
in both instances a 'Japanese' simulacrum is only asserted by virtue
of its reproduction of West Lake before 1945, of Shukkei-en after 1945.

After one line spoken by the narrator, the survivor continues her
memories: 'I was weak and my skin hung from my fingertips like
cloth.' Together they stroll through the garden, calling the carp to the
surface of the water. They stop to use the restroom: 'So she began as
we squatted over the toilets.' Such an open reference to the sterility of
the lower bodily stratum and its excretory function transgresses the
bounds of poetic decorum. The reader is warned, in a sense, that this
will be a graphic poem that does not shrink from the physical. The
image lends a sense of corporeality to the survivor's words: 'If you
want, I'll tell you, but nothing I say will be enough. / We tried to dress
our burns with vegetable oil.' It seems as though the memories themselves do not cause as much pain as the possibility that her words will
not faithfully speak the memories. The pathos of victims using such
simple kitchen salves for such brutal wounds is heightened because
the survivor leads us to expect something transcendental; instead she
tries to explain in the simplest – most pathetic – terms possible. A few
lines later, her description becomes even more graphic: 'I don't like
this particular red flower because / it reminds me of a woman's brain
crushed under a roof.' She leaves nothing to the imagination in this
frank, explicit image of the horrors of atomic warfare.

It is at this point in 'The Garden Shukkei-en' as the narrator and
survivor stroll in the garden, as the survivor is carried away by the
power of a garden to seduce memory, that the survivor recalls herself
and says, 'Perhaps my language is too precise, and therefore difficult

91

to understand?' The remaining five lines of the poem (spoken by the survivor) contain no physical description of carnage or destruction whatsoever. She retreats from the brutality. The rest of the poem is about approximations, about representations and their failure to live up to reality: 'We have not, all these years, felt what you call happiness. / But at times, with good fortune, we experience something close. / As our life resembles life, and this garden the garden.' The approximation of happiness is compared to the resemblance of this garden to the garden of 1945, that was in its inception a reproduction. The survivor could point to no more powerful symbol of the fragility of representation than the restored shukkei-en.

Once drawn in, those who write about history in gardens are denied retreat from the inescapable forces of the anxiety of representation. (This could explain why Vergil walked away from writing about gardens in the *Georgics*.) The survivor – and ultimately the poet – knows that the representation of the events will fall short of the reality it attempts to portray. In a speech to the people about the Bacchanalian conspiracy, Livy eloquently stated the historian's – and the poet's – and the survivor's – problem: 'Whatever I shall have said, be sure that my words are less than the dreadfulness and gravity of the situation' (Livy 39.15.5). The historian is not unaware that the text he creates is insufficient to portray events realistically. Rhetoric falls like a veil over the past, rendering it palpable even as it distorts. I hazard that Tacitus, student and practitioner of oratory, was aware of the duplicity of rhetoric. The moments of his self-consciousness and the intrusion of the first person betray the anxiety of representation. No doubt such fear that representation will fall short of reality is implicit in any literary production; yet the will to represent remains unquenchable. If the *Annals* fails to represent the past faithfully, it succeeds in reminding us of our fallibility and finitude. How Augustine (a man torn between two women) handles these very shortcomings in his autobiographical *Confessions* is the subject of our next chapter.

The Garden of Redemption

The art of gardening is like the art of writing, of
painting, of sculpture; it is the art of composing, and
making a harmony, with disparate elements.

Ian Hamilton Finlay

I

In 397 CE in the town of Hippo in North Africa, a forty-three-year-old
bishop named Aurelius Augustinus set out to write the story of his
conversion to the Christian faith some ten years before. In narrating
his life, from his infancy and childhood through puberty and his adult
years, he gives an extraordinary picture of what it was like to grow up
in provincial Roman North Africa, to be educated in Carthage, to be a
schoolteacher at Rome, and a professor of rhetoric at Milan. The result
is a unique document for social history, filled with details about daily
life in late antiquity and offering rare glimpses of the breast-feeding
mother, the father and son at the baths, the disobedient schoolboy, the
hyper-hormonal teenager, the overworked schoolteacher, the bereft
friend, the grieving son. These details, however, are incidental to the
psychological purpose of the *Confessions*; indeed such concrete, physical details are included for the purpose of lending credibility to the
spiritual, and thereby intangible, transformation at the heart of the
narrative. Augustine seeks not so much to recount the details of his
life, as to recollect and reconstruct the journey by which he arrived at
a moment that profoundly transformed his mental and spiritual state
of being. To this end, Augustine's life and *Confessions* lead to one
point: his conversion in the garden in Milan.

Augustine begins *Confessions* Book 8 by recounting his visit in
Milan to a friend named Simplicianus, the spiritual father of Ambrose,
who was bishop of Milan and a powerful influence on Augustine.
Simplicianus told Augustine a story of the conversion of Marius

Victorinus, a successful teacher at Rome who was a practising pagan until his public declaration of faith in the full sight of the assembled faithful (8.2). This story inspired Augustine all the more to imitate the convert. One day, Augustine and his friend Alypius were visited by a fellow African named Ponticianus, a Christian with whom they had a long conversation. Ponticianus told them a story about the conversion of three men at Trier. One afternoon, he and his three companions went out to stroll in the gardens near the city walls. They became separated into two groups of two. As they wandered, the second pair came to a house, in which the owners had a book of the life of Antony, an Egyptian monk. Upon reading the inspiring biography, they converted (8.6). Thus, stories of conversion are embedded within conversations. Furthermore, the exemplary life story of Antony is embedded within a story about conversion, which is in turn embedded in a conversation.

Augustine goes on to describe the torment of his soul and the divisions that plagued him: 'My inner self was a house divided against itself' (8.8.19). Distraught after years of searching for truth and not finding consolation for his aching soul, Augustine finally removed himself from the company of his friends to weep in a garden:

> Our host had a small garden, which we used just as we used the rest of the estate, for the host, the master of the house, was not living there. The turmoil in my breast had driven me out of that house to that place, where no one could interrupt that burning struggle which I was waging with myself, until it reached its conclusion (8.8.19).

Thus, at the beginning of the episode, Augustine withdraws to the garden seeking solitude. He continues:

> [... its conclusion] which you knew, but I did not. But I was raving in a healthy way and I was dying in life, aware of what evil I was and unaware of what good I would be a little later (8.8.19).

The switch to the second person reminds the reader caught up in the narrative of the life story that the *Confessions* is in form a sort of conversation between the author and God: 'The book's most pervasive

94

bit of artifice makes mortal readers irrelevant,' says O'Donnell in his recent biography of Augustine (2005, 77). Furthermore, the effect of the first oxymoron is heightened by the interlocking word order: *insaniebam salubriter et moriebar vitaliter* and reinforced by the second antinomy: *gnarus quid mali ... ignarus quid boni.* Augustine puts the contradictions that typify the rhetoric of the garden to good use in his description of his incipient conversion. Finally, the end of the sentence reminds the reader of the temporal distance between 'then' and 'now,' between the moment in the garden and its attendant circumstance of ignorance, and the moment of writing carried out in full knowledge. The whole sentence strikes me as incredibly efficient, bringing forward major themes – conversion, conversation, paradox, and temporality – with minimal adornment.

In his exhaustive and unsurpassed commentary on the *Confessions*, O'Donnell demonstrates the ways that at this point, the narrative of conversion proceeds to operate on two levels at once. Augustine describes his restless physical gestures and at the same time reveals the inner psychological monologue that accompanied them. In a 'binocular vision,' Augustine's words express what he might have uttered at the time in his interior monologue, and what he, at the time of writing the *Confessions*, utters in perplexity (O'Donnell 1992 *ad* 8.9.21). Such bipartite structure readily returns the narrative to one final refutation of Manicheism, the gnostic faith that Augustine had professed for nine years, from which he sought to distance himself once and for all. The dualism of Manichean teaching with its permanent dichotomies between good and evil, mind and flesh, light and dark, hounded Augustine (whose polemic provided a lopsided view of this lost religion until the discovery of the Mani Codex in 1969). Throughout the *Confessions*, one senses in Augustine a hint of embarrassment, or at least a need to minimize his affiliation with this controversial sect (O'Donnell 2005, 53).

Augustine had entered the garden with his friend Alypius, but when his emotions became too much to bear, he retreated further, leaving his friend behind (8.12.28). He flung himself to the ground before a fig tree and gave himself over to sobbing,

> with the most bitter grief of my heart, when *ecce* – behold – I hear
> a sound from the nearby house, a chant repeated over and over,

whether by a boy or girl I do not know, saying 'take, read; take, read' (8.12.29).

Remembering how Antony had converted after hearing the Gospel by chance, and taking the chant as a personal address to himself, Augustine believed that these words were an injunction to read Scripture. He quickly returned to Alypius, for he had left a copy of Paul's Epistles there. Augustine took up the Letter to the Romans and read in silence the first verse his eyes happened upon. Immediately upon reading the chance sentence from the epistle, the light of confidence flooded his heart and all doubts and hesitations dispersed. The moment in the garden is the dramatic climax to years of soul-searching, self-doubt and even self-hatred. His tortured soul finds God in a garden of conversion.

II

Upon his conversion, Augustine resigned his position as professor of rhetoric in Milan. It was the time of the Vintage Holidays (the *Feriae Vindemiales*, coincidentally the same pagan festival celebrated by Messalina and her lover Silius) and Augustine with an assortment of friends retreated to a friend's country villa at Cassiacum (about 40 km or 25 miles north of Milan), where he wrote several treatises before his baptism back in Milan. With the conversion completed, he decided to return to Africa with his mother Monica, who had joined him in Italy two years before. Together they travelled to Ostia, the port of Rome, to await their passage to Africa. Augustine recounts their last conversation together:

> Not long before the day on which she was to die (you knew, but we were ignorant), … she and I stood alone, looking out a certain window from which we had a view of the garden in the courtyard of the house where we were staying in Ostia, where we rested up, after the long journey to this point, for the voyage [to Africa] (9.10.23).

Once again, the abrupt change to the second person makes the mortal reader 'irrelevant,' as Augustine converses with God and the reader is reduced to the status of eavesdropper. The adjective *soli* is somewhat paradoxical. Between solitude and communion mother and son are together, and alone. As in the scene in the garden in Milan, Augustine calls attention to the temporal gap between the event and his narration of the event, again framed in terms of his ignorance and God's knowledge.

Monica and Augustine spoke of eternal wisdom and the love of God that surpasses all physical pleasure. Although Augustine is unable to recount the exact words of their conversation, nevertheless he carefully and accurately conveys to the reader the serene and joyful emotions evoked in this garden of conversation. Five days later, Monica succumbed to a fever and died.

I began this chapter by asserting that the *Confessions* reaches a conclusion in the conversion scene in Book 8; however, five more books follow before the autobiography ends. Why does Augustine not conclude with his conversion? Or with his baptism? Or with the death of his mother at the end of Book 9? Book 10 (and especially 10.8-25) is an essay on memory, which might seem superfluous, except that the entire enterprise of the *Confessions* depends upon Augustine's memory, its abilities, and its selectiveness. Memory, as an act of recollection, is the medium that makes autobiography possible, even as it simultaneously ensures that the autobiography will always be incomplete. Book 11 (especially 11.14-31) is a discourse on time, equally difficult to define, and presumably superfluous, except that the repeated disjuncture of past and present likewise shapes and directs the course of the *Confessions*. 'Therefore, what is time? If no one asks me, I know; if I wish to explain it to someone who asks, I do not' (11.14.17). Thus, in Books 10 and 11, Augustine confronts possible objections to his authority by addressing memory and time directly. In the last two books, then, he proffers allegorical readings and interpretations of the book of Genesis in order to demonstrate how to make the temporary into the permanent, thereby sealing his conversion.

*Con*version and *con*versation – both effect profound transformation, from sin to virtue, from death to life, from the ephemeral to the eternal. Although etymologically both nouns derive from the Latin verb *vertere* (to turn), conversation contains in its suffix the frequentative form denoting forcible or repeated action. While this frequentative force has no doubt faded from the quotidian usage of the noun 'conversation,' nevertheless the prefix *con-* in both conversation and conversion carries a sense of community and social interaction. Conversation requires the immediate company of others; conversion demands that changes, often undertaken in solitude, be upheld permanently in the company of others. To reach the point of confession (note the recurrent prefix), Augustine demonstrates the desperate need for the social intercourse of immediate conversation and permanent conversion.

This tension between the momentary and the permanent is but one of the many psychological fault lines or fissures along which the author of the *Confessions* dwells precipitously. Augustine lived on the edge, in a world between worlds, between Christian and pagan religions, between Punic and Latin languages, indeed between classical and medieval Latin, between the influences of the distant city of Rome and the local, provincial home town, between the political stability of the longest lasting empire of the ancient Mediterranean and its imminent sack by Alaric and the Goths. Somehow, he did not fall through these cracks. Instead, he seems to have thrived in the interstices.

Indeed, his description of God begins with superlatives but swiftly falls into antithesis, whereby God dwells in the gap:

> God highest, best, most powerful, most all knowing, most merciful and most just, most mysterious and most manifest, most beautiful and most brave, most steadfast and most incomprehensible, never changing but changing all, never new, never old, renewing all things and humiliating the proud, always engaged, always at rest, gathering and yet not lacking, carrying and filling and protecting, creating and nourishing and perfecting, seeking though you lack nothing. You love but not overly passionately, you are jealous yet without care, you repent but do not feel sorry, you grow angry and yet remain calm, you change your deeds but not your intention, you take back what you have lost and yet you have never lost anything; you are never in need and still you rejoice in profit, you are never greedy but still you collect interest (1.4.4).

Recall that in Frances and Hester (1990, 4, above p. 17), this kind of antithesis contributes to a sense of disjointed prose, one of the hallmarks of the rhetoric of garden literature. In exploring the disparity in conceptual analysis of gardens, Elkins identifies a range of conceptual schemata, or ways of thinking about gardens. For instance, we have seen how gardens may be represented in terms of polarities (Elkins 1993, 190, above p. 16). In this passage from the *Confessions*, God, like the garden, is also conceived of as a set of polarities.

Furthermore, according to Elkins, gardens also make good metaphors for life narratives, in which 'the central image is life's course and the ways gardens reflect or facilitate it' (1993, 191). As the site of conversation and conversion, the garden is a central metaphor in the *Confessions*. The garden is a place onto which Augustine can map an organic narrative of his life from infancy to conversion, with imagery of growth and decay, fertility and sterility, inclusion and exclusion. Augustine's antithetical description of God prepares the ground, so to speak, for the sowing of a fertile garden metaphor by means of what Hunt calls 'the Eden effect'. The Garden of Eden exists only in the descriptions, the words and images of those who were there originally or in the accounts of those who can only visit it in their imaginations: 'Everybody could make Eden in his or her own image, simply because the original was not there to confront and confound their particular theory' (2004, 27). Just as it is impossible to gainsay a description of Eden by visiting the place, so there is no empirical evidence to counter Augustine's individual version of God.

Antithesis, however, has its price. Augustine was divided, he tells us in Book 8, between two wills, 'one old, the other new, this one physical, this one spiritual; they fought among themselves and in their conflict they ripped my soul apart' (8.5.10). In the time just before conversion, his soul sinks into profound depths of self-hatred, and he provides perhaps one of the most painful descriptions of psychological alienation (see O'Donnell 1992 *ad* 8.7.16):

With your words, Lord, you twisted me back upon myself … you set me before my own face that I might see how vile I was, how disfigured and filthy, how filled with blemishes and sores. And I saw, and I was horrified, and I had no place to escape myself (8.7.16).

Such self-deprecation and even self-flagellation (see especially 8.7.18,

99

'with what whips did I not flagellate my soul?') perhaps offend modern sensibilities. But for those put off by the physicality of Augustine's mental anguish, he also offers a much more subtle, and succinct, description of his life on the edge: 'I was one who desired, I was one who did not desire: I was' (8.10.22). Whether one likes it or not, at least Augustine is capable of stating his position. When the scale refuses to tip in favour of one state of being over the other, Augustine simply resigns. *Ego eram* destroys the need to choose. Both alternatives are dismissed because it is impossible (or embarrassing, or dangerous, or finally meaningless) to choose between them. In such an interpretive situation, according to Barthes, 'one no longer needs to choose, but only to endorse' (1972, 153). And my sense is that if there is one thing Augustine would wish more than anything to avoid, it is choice.

Moreover, in this simple formulation, 'I was one who desired, I was one who did not: I was,' we can glimpse one of the earliest formulations of a cornerstone of what Althusser calls 'Christian religious ideology', namely, the individual's recognition of himself as subject and his acceptance of subjugation (1971, 177-81). Outmoded though Althusserian Marxism may be, it nonetheless lets us apprehend yet another fissure in Augustinian existence. *Eram*: I was. Augustine carries this past existence with him. Yet when God spoke to Moses, he said, 'I am who am,' *ego sum qui sum*, present tense. Eternal God resides in the present tense; the mortal Augustine is trapped in the past. And yet the act of writing his *Confessions* converts all that was past into the present, so that the entire enterprise of self-writing, that is, autobiography, mediates the disjuncture. Augustine's *eram* is written from the perspective of one who has accepted God's *sum*.

Augustine lives between two worlds; he resides on the edges, metaphorically, physically, and emotionally. The garden in Milan may have been the most important garden in Augustine's life, but it was not the last to effect a profound transformation on the development of his character – nor was it the first.

III

Augustine was born in the small town of Thagaste in North Africa, where he attended his first school. When he was about eleven years old, he was sent to Madaura, about twenty miles from Thagaste, where

100

he studied literature and the art of public speaking for five years. At the age of sixteen, he was brought back home so that his father Patricius, 'a modest citizen of Thagaste' could save up the tuition to send him further afield to Carthage (2.3.5). A teenage boy cut loose from school, Augustine idled away his days in the company of rough-necks. Augustine recounts a particular prank:

> There was a pear tree near our vineyard, loaded with fruit that was attractive neither to look at nor to taste. We worthless punks (*adulescentuli*) went off to shake down the fruit and carry it away late one night, until which time we had continued our sport in the yard in our usual pernicious way. We made off with an enormous load, not to eat them ourselves, but simply to throw them to the pigs. Perhaps we ate some of them, but it became for us something pleasing because it was not allowed (2.4.9).

The language here is laden with echoes from Sallust's account of the conspiracy of Catiline, whose wickedness is referred to explicitly in the next paragraph (2.5.11). For example, Sallust uses the contemptuous word *adulescentuli*, or 'worthless punks,' twice of Catiline's conspira-tors, as does Cicero in his oration against Catiline (*Against Catiline* 1.6.13). The temporal setting, *nocte intempesta*, 'late at night', also recalls the preferred hour of criminals and conspirators. According to O'Donnell, however, the phrase means something slightly different among Christians, for whom it denotes loneliness 'marked by both vulnerability and possibility' (O'Donnell 1992 *ad* 2.4.9). It seems that Augustine's use of the phrase moves between the two connotations; as we shall see, his ability to meld the pagan and Christian worlds gives his writing its unique force.

This seemingly harmless episode provokes three pages on the na-ture of evil and becomes the paradigm of sinfulness and the dark side of human nature. In a footnote, Brown tucks away a quotation from Oliver Wendell Holmes: 'Rum thing to see a man making a mountain out of robbing a peartree in his teens' (2000, 166n.4). Why does this episode command so much space in the *Confessions*? In his essay, 'Truth in Autobiography', Coetzee describes an 'economy of confession', in which 'everything shameful is valuable' (1984.3). What are these pears worth to Augustine, to his endeavour to tell his life story?

101

Perhaps an explanation can be found if we consider the act of stealing fruit from the perspective of Manicheism, which taught that the universe was composed of an amalgam of two principles, the one good, spiritual, and light, the other evil, corporeal, and dark. The elect members of the sect were forbidden from preparing their own food. They could not reap plants or slaughter animals. These duties were performed for them by the hearers, or the common members who aspired to become elect. So, the plucking of fruit was, for a Manichee, a sin. By feeding the pears to swine (instead of bringing it to the elect), Augustine increased his sinfulness (Ferrari 1970, 235-7). Yet why should this infraction of Manichean ethics matter, when the point of the *Confessions* is for Augustine to distance himself from this objectionable sect and to narrate his conversion toward Christianity?

Perhaps then we should seek an explanation for the lengthy discourse on the pear-theft in Christian mythology. Adam's sin was to pluck the fruit of the Tree of Knowledge of Good and Evil in the Garden of Eden. The fall and redemption of humankind are recast in the *Confessions* as Augustine recounts his redemption in the garden in Milan. So perhaps the pear tree, a site of great sinfulness, has as its narrative doublet the fig tree beneath which Augustine wept and experienced his conversion (on 'arboreal polarization' see Ferrari 1970 and 1979).

Augustine does offer a reason: He is disturbed because he stole not out of necessity or even want, but out of the sheer satisfaction of doing wrong. Bear in mind that his remorse is that of a forty-three-year-old convert looking back in retrospect on his youth. It is highly unlikely that the sixteen-year-old boy felt shame or regret as he was running away from the pillaged pear tree. This kind of temporal 'jet-lag' characterizes the *Confessions*. The time of the event in the narrative (the pears are stolen in 369) is telescoped with the time of literary production (the *Confessions* are written in 397), between which the most momentous event of Augustine's life – his conversion – takes place (386). Such temporal disjunction easily escapes the notice of the reader engrossed in the confession of the pear theft. Such temporal disjunction also gives the *Confessions* a sense of timelessness. Augustine has robbed the pear-theft of its place in time so that it can become an event for all ages, that is, a myth, devoid of particularity so as to become universal.

4. The Garden of Redemption

In contrast to the minimal adornment elsewhere in the *Confessions*, three weighty literary devices gild the episode of the pear theft: foreshadowing, allusion, and synecdoche. The pear theft in the neighbour's garden prepares the ground for Augustine's own conversion in the garden in Milan. The former arouses anxiety over the nature of sin; the latter puts an end to all sinful anxiety. The conversion in Milan inverts the theft of the pears. As a boy, he steals something forbidden although he has no need for the fruit. As a man, he receives something given to him by the grace of God, something he needs more than anything in the world. We have already seen an easy allusion to the Garden of Eden. In Eden, Adam and Eve enter the garden and steal forbidden fruit. Their actions separate them from God. As Adam and Eve become aware of their sexuality upon eating the fruit, so Augustine at the age of sixteen has clearly entered puberty (he recounts this earlier in Book 2). By synecdoche, the pear theft comes to stand for all of Augustine's other, unnamed sins, and in particular, his sexual indiscretions. By confessing this one rather innocuous sin, he can confess, without naming, far more insidious and perverted acts. The pear theft scarcely compares to the unspoken deeds left to the reader's imagination.

We can read the pears as symbolic of all the women with whom Augustine had illicit sex: they were not particularly pretty or pleasing, and when he was finished with them he threw them to the swine. In this case, by means of the pear theft Augustine confesses his lost innocence and despairs of his separation from God. Lost innocence and separation are themes reminiscent of pastoral poetry; according to O'Donnell, loss is likewise a major theme of the *Confessions* (2005, 76). In Vergil's *Eclogue* 8, the shepherd Damon sings of the despair of a jilted lover. He recalls the wistful memory of the lover's first glimpse of his girl:

> Within our garden hedge I saw you, I was guide for both, a little child along with my mother, plucking dewy apples. My eleventh year finished, the next had just greeted me; from the ground I could now reach the frail boughs. As I saw, how I was lost! How wicked a mistake bore me away! (8.37-41).

The lover only having just reached maturity plucks fruit within the walls of a garden when he experiences loss. At the same time that he realizes his lost innocence, he despairs of the separation of the girl from his sight, his grasp, his possession. Wedded in Augustine's account of the pear theft are images of both Eden and the *Eclogues*.

This is the hallmark of Augustine's thought: the ability to craft an artful, memorable scene from elements that are simultaneously drawn from both the Judaeo-Christian and the classical pagan mythologies. For example, in the beginning of the *Confessions* Augustine laments that his early education was based on pagan literature and not Christian scripture: 'praise of you, through your scriptures, should have supported the vine-shoot of my heart.' He continues to say that 'it would not have been snatched away through the emptiness of trifles as the shameful spoil of birds' (1.17.27). Augustine grafts the echo of the Gospel of John, 'I am the vine and you are the branches' (15.4) onto a reference from Vergil's *Georgics* (2.60) in which inferior fruit is carried off by birds (see Clark 1995, 112). Thus it is curious that Vergil, who declined to write about the garden, so deeply permeated the thought of Augustine, for whom the garden is a powerful locus (for the presence of Vergil in the works of Augustine, see the superb study by MacCormack 1998).

Some conclusions emerge. First, the garden is, for Augustine, good to think with; it serves as an organic metaphor for important moments in the narrative of his life. Secondly, although Augustine lived in a radically different world from Horace and Tacitus, nevertheless for all three writers, the garden maintains a powerful hold on the literary imagination. Perhaps this hold is nowhere better demonstrated than in a willingness to accept Augustine's narration of his conversion in a garden at face value. The historicity of the garden in Milan does not concern us here; rather, the garden, whether by historical coincidence or by fictional authorial choice, is a central metaphor throughout the *Confessions*. Nevertheless, the problem of historicity demonstrates the way that the garden shapes perceptions.

Most who read the garden scene in *Confessions* 8 have little reason to doubt that Augustine recounts events that occurred. But some maintain that the episode is fictionalized; Augustine did not retreat to a garden, did not fall at the foot of a fig tree, did not hear children's voices chanting. Or if he did, such simple actions could not have provoked such a profound effect (see Courcelle 1950, 188-202; 1963,

191-7; O'Meara 1965, 183-5). After a review of the debate, Ferrari reiterates his position that Augustine underwent not one, but a series of conversions, and that the garden scene in Milan is but one step in the process leading to complete change (1984, 50; 1989, 246-7; 2003 is his most explicit assertion of the fictionality of the scene). In criticizing scholars who argue for the historicity of the scene, Ferrari speaks of Courcelle, who 'still seemed under the spell of the powerful conversion scene', and of the 'influence of the spell', and 'breaking the spell of the justly famous conversion scene' (1989, 246). When Elkins asserts that 'gardens are like mild soporifics, inducing a certain frame of mind or habit of thought, over which we have limited control' (1993, 196), he cogently describes the effect that the garden in Milan continues to have for readers of the *Confessions*. There is no reason to complain of this, but only to ask for candour.

IV

We have seen that Augustine's life was characterized by what Brown calls a 'heroic endurance of unresolved tensions' (2000, 371). For O'Donnell, the *Confessions* is characterized by a duality in content: 'One book, two readings, theological and autobiographical. ... Curiously and appropriately enough, the fault line that separates the *Confessions*-about-god and the *Confessions*-about-Augustine runs right through the most vividly remembered scene of the book, the one in the garden in Milan' (2005, 63). I would like to plumb the depths of the possible ways that gardens and autobiographies also embody certain tensions or even contradictions. First, the autobiographer attempts to integrate the fragments of lived experience in order to reconstruct a unified totality (Gusdorf 1980, 37-8; O'Donnell 2005, 84). So too the gardener, as Ian Hamilton Finlay remarks, makes harmony with disparate elements.

Second, both gardens and autobiographies are the results of both cyclical and teleological causes. The garden, existing from season to season, is a cyclical phenomenon, in a permanent state of becoming. The garden also strives for a form determined by its executor: gardeners have a plan, a purpose, and an end toward which they strive. The life that is the subject of the autobiography likewise cyclically recapitulates its existence in the passing of time under the seasons. But the life also reaches its telos in death, ultimately. For the autobiography, the life reaches an end co-terminous with the end of the narrative (which, ironically, can never be co-terminous with the death of the author). The gardener and the autobiographer both mediate the cyclical and teleological aspects of their subject.

A third fissure runs through both the garden and the autobiography: both dwell between being and becoming. Both are never finished; both are always in the making, in the doing (on autobiography, see the seminal essay by Gusdorf 1980, 47). The temporal perspective of the autobiography is necessarily retrospective. The author is always one looking back on his past. Yet writing autobiography brings the past into the present. That person 'then' is being described by this person 'now,' and the act of writing collapses the temporal distance between the two. Likewise for gardens, temporal perspectives seem to be telescoped together or to interpenetrate one another. The garden too is a place where 'then' and 'now' coalesce.

A greater contradiction plagues both the garden and the autobiography: the problem of self-presentation. The gardener manipulates plants and their growth so that they appear more 'natural' than nature would have them. Likewise, the autobiographer controls his own self-image to such a degree that no reader would dare take the writer at face value. This is the premise upon which O'Donnell's biography of Augustine appears to be predicated: a 'competing narrative lies behind the story of the *Confessions*. Whatever we come away believing, we must be made to forget the hostile counternarrative' (2005, 52). O'Donnell operates under the assumption that Augustine is constantly struggling to create a self-image intended to defeat what others thought of him.

To be effective, the autobiographer must constantly earn the reader's confidence in his struggle for credibility. In this sense, I find autobiography to be one of the most pernicious forms of self-presentation, for I wonder, who enforces the ethics of autobiography? How easily can a reader be led down the garden path by an author who purports to tell his whole life, blemishes and all? Yet what autobiographer would confess to unspeakable crimes to the extent of self-condemnation? How can the reader be sure that crimes confessed were in fact committed? Furthermore, to what extent can the autobiographer manipulate representations of *other* persons in his life? If it is acceptable to alter events and persons so as to lend narrative unity and cohesion to the written life, is it likewise acceptable to alter events and persons for *other* reasons? Perhaps most disturbing, as Coetzee (1984) points out, is to ask what right a reader has to question the autobiographer's authenticity or sincerity? Surely the autobiographer takes as much, if not more, of a risk than the reader?

Here we depart from a comparison of gardens to autobiography, to a second level of comparison, between representations of gardens, that is, gardens in the literary imagination, and autobiography. For when read in the context of the classical, pagan gardens of Columella, Tacitus, and especially Horace, the gardens in Augustine's *Confessions* provide instructive similarities and differences.

Obviously, the garden scene in Milan bears little resemblance to the garden of Columella's didactic poem. If we accept that the conversion actually took place in a garden as Augustine describes, it is perhaps closer to Tacitus' representation of the Gardens of Lucullus; both the Milanese and Lucullan gardens were real places, and the events that took place in them were narrated for a particular historical purpose. To the extent that the garden in Horace *Satire* 1.8 had a footing in reality, it offers perhaps the best comparison. Like Augustine's conversion narrative, it is written in the first person. When taken together, *Satire* 1.8 and the conversion scene in *Confessions* 8 let us apprehend something of the power of the garden to articulate discord, whereby enchantment mediates conflict.

Recall the opening of *Satire* 1.8 with its distinction between 'then' and 'now'. A similar temporal disjunction pervades the *Confessions*, according to Brown, with its palpable 'tension between the "then" of the young man and the "now" of the bishop' (2000,157). The Priapus of *Satire* 1.8 is a fiction. He is a character created by the poet to meet his narratological needs. Priapus expresses an anxiety about his position within the garden and his ability to fend off intruders and transgressors. Horace puts this face on his poetry in part to shield himself from accusations of opportunism. The Augustine of *Confessions* 8 is, to a certain extent, likewise a fiction. He is a character created by the author to meet his narratological needs. He expresses an anxiety about his position within a metaphorical garden and his ability as a newly converted Christian to fend off not only intruders and transgressors, but to keep in check his own misbehaviour. In the move that

107

inaugurates autobiography, Augustine internalizes some of the kinds of problems that the vexed poet Horace externalized when he made Priapus the spokesman of his poem.

Toward the end of his career, Horace (accurately, so it would seem) predicts the fate of his book of poetry, that it will someday become a textbook: 'This too awaits you, that stammering old age will keep you busy teaching boys the basics in some remote village' (*Epistles* 1.20.17-18). Likewise anticipating the responses of later generations of readers, Augustine in his old age composed the *Reconsiderations*, an annotated bibliography listing his own works. According to O'Donnell, we should not underestimate the importance of this seemingly pedantic encyclopaedia (2005, 317-19), for in it, Augustine gets the last word on how, and why, we should read the *Confessions*:

> Thirteen books of my *Confessions*, which praise the just and good God in all my evil and good ways, and stir up towards Him the mind and feelings of men: as far as I am concerned, they had this effect on me when I wrote them, and they still do this, when now I read them. What others think is their own business: I know at least, that many of the brethren have enjoyed them, and still do (*Reconsiderations* 2.32, in Brown 2000, 434-5).

Authors would like very much indeed to control how their works are read. Very few succeed like Augustine.

In their narratives of gardens, Columella, Horace, and Tacitus reach moments when they recall themselves from the reverie generated by the garden's sumptuous pleasures. Vergil declines to engage in representing the garden. Columella reels in his inclination to allow the garden to run away with his senses. Horace's Priapus stops himself from describing the witches in too much detail. Tacitus intrudes upon the narrative in a first-person assertion that robs the garden of its power to lead the author astray. In each instance, these Roman authors openly exercise self-control when narrating gardens. How striking then, to see Augustine (and every reader thereafter) allow himself to be fully transported and transformed – and redeemed – in and by the garden.

V

In 'Truth in Autobiography,' Coetzee speaks of the 'gaps and evasions, perhaps even the lies' that make up a life story (1984, 4). Take, for example, this description:

> Always, when he tried to explain himself to himself, there remained a gap, a hole, a darkness before which his understanding balked, into which it was useless to pour words. The words were eaten up, the gap remained. His was always a story with a hole in it: a wrong story, always wrong.

Although this sounds like a description of the futility that an autobiographer must overcome, it is taken not from an autobiography, but from Coetzee's novel, *Life & Times of Michael K* (p. 110). This twentieth-century work of literature throws into sharp relief Augustine's monolithic, redemptive garden of Milan.

Set during a civil war, *Life & Times of Michael K* is about a destitute, disaffected, and disfranchised South African man and his journey from the crowded metropolis of Cape Town to the countryside in the Karoo, the elevated, arid plateau in the centre of Cape Province. K is a gardener in the city, and when his mother falls ill with dropsy, she asks her only son to take her home, to the farm where she grew up as a girl working for the white owners. On the way, the mother dies in Stellenbosch, so K's journey takes on new purpose: to bury his mother's ashes. K finds the farm, or what may be the farm, abandoned by the white owners. K lives there without money and without any sort of social intercourse, rejecting the shelter of the farmhouse and out- buildings and instead eating and sleeping and filling all of his bodily needs on the veldt. He finds and plants pumpkin seeds, which he tenderly cultivates and pathetically consumes. He is frightened off the land by an army deserter and is subsequently picked up and commandeered for a forced labour camp, from which he escapes. He returns to the farm which is then visited by guerrillas. He escapes the insurgents only to be captured by the army. He is mistaken as a sympathizer who was growing food for the rebels and is kept in a 'rehabilitation' camp back in Cape Town. He manages to escape the camp and to return to the neighbourhood where his mother used to

109

live and work. Resisting all closure, the novel ends with K imagining survival on teaspoons of water.

Part 1 relates K's journey to the Karoo and his capture. Part 3 serves as a sort of epilogue, describing K's return to the neighbourhood in Cape Town where the story began. In between, Part 2 interrupts the flow of this third-person narrative, with a radical shift in point of view, to a first-person narration by a medical officer in the rehabilitation camp. And this first-person narrative further devolves into free indirect discourse.

Throughout Part 2, the medical officer is continually and utterly frustrated by K's evasive existence, beginning with his name. In the rehabilitation camp, the enigmatic initial K that stands for some undesignated surname (that is never revealed) is cast aside, and K is mislabelled 'Michaels' in a futile attempt to identify this nameless man (the debate on the symbolism of the initial K begins with Gordimer 1998, 139; Dovey 1988, 267; Merivale 1996; Attridge 2004, 51). Brought into the camp in a state of starvation, K nevertheless refuses to eat. The medical officer cannot understand K's refusal of nourishment; his starvation threatens to bring the entire novel to a halt. If K dies, the story effectively ends (in fact, in the end, K does not die, thereby denying the novel a logical conclusion). Why can K not comprehend the need to sustain himself? Is he so simple, so stupid?

Part 2 ends with a five-page tirade, which takes place entirely in the thoughts of the medical officer. Now that K has escaped the camp, what would happen if the medical officer were to escape as well, to leave his post, pursue, and apprehend K? He imagines the scenario and the ensuing encounter. In the medical officer's strident demands for meaning, one can sense the reader/critic likewise demanding to know from the author just what this evasive novel means:

> Did you not notice how, whenever I tried to pin you down, you slipped away? I noticed. Do you know what thought crossed my mind when I saw you had got away without cutting the wire? 'He must be a polevaulter' – that is what I thought. Well, you may not be a polevaulter, Michaels, but you are a great escape artist, one of the great escapees: I take my hat off to you! (p. 166)

As the medical officer is simultaneously frustrated and amazed by K's

110

ability to resist and even escape meaning, so the reader, no doubt frustrated by this point with this cryptically allegorical novel will likewise stand in awe of Coetzee's ability to resist interpretation. In this sense, we can anticipate (in the next chapter) the critical guidance that the playwright Stoppard will give his audience, in more subtle and, in keeping with the purpose of metatheatre, more entertaining ways. Coetzee makes manifest the frustration that the reader has with this puzzling novel, and in this metafictional move, he writes into the novel the fact that 'any story, once told, is subject to consumption by a critical society' (Heider 1993, 96).

Marais effectively demonstrates the ways that the novel operates on a metafictional plane and the effects that this self-reflexivity has on interpretation. By calling attention to the act of writing, Coetzee betrays the linguistic medium and advertises the fact that K and his experience is created in and by language. The second part of the novel, with its striking shift in point of view, emphasizes a 'self-conscious foregrounding of language' (Marais 2001,114). Thus the novel demonstrates the possibility for language to tell a story, but at the same time, 'the text self-consciously describes the inevitable failure of writing' (2001, 120).

Coetzee is not alone in recognizing the achievement as well as the failure of artistic representation. In the last chapter, I tried to excavate Tacitus' particular awareness of this paradox. But given my quest for the garden in the Roman literary imagination, I am inclined to return to the *Georgics*, again, the poem in which the garden is conspicuous by its absence. In his commentary on the *Georgics*, Thomas identifies two central themes, 'that of failure before the resurgent forces of the natural world, and of success which is tainted by a spiritual failure' (Thomas 1988, 21). The two themes merge at the end of the poem in the retelling of the myth of Orpheus, the Thracian bard who successfully charmed his way into the Underworld to retrieve his beloved Eurydice. He is permitted to bring her back, provided he does not look upon her until they reach the land of the living. But on the ascent, he is seized by an uncontrollable passion to look at her (*Georgics* 4.488), and stopping on the very threshold of light in a 'no-man's land' between life and death, he looks back. As soon as he sees her, he loses her forever. Vergil's version of the myth, with the ruinous backward glance, allegorizes the relationship between poet and oeuvre. Once a work is created and given to the world, the poet no longer has any control over how it will be received. Augustine knew this, of course, and so scripted a response to his works in his *Reconsiderations*. For Marais, the metafiction in *Life & Times of Michael K* comes down to a matter of control. With self-reflexive assertions of the 'radical and uncontrollable ambiguity of writing', Coetzee is able to *assert* control over the ambiguity. 'Is not this staging of writing as a realm in which control slips away, perversely, itself an attempt at control?' (Marais 2001, 122). So, I wonder, when Vergil declines to write about the garden, self-consciously objecting to the difficulty and admitting defeat, does he not also, at the same time, assert a degree of control over the intractable garden?

We have come a long way from Columella's poem about how to cultivate a garden. From this poem in which the garden figures prominently as the subject and the poet's sole concern, we advanced to Horace's poem about the transformation of a garden and the transgressions that occurred in it. In Tacitus and Augustine, the garden was no longer the subject but the setting for moments of transgression and transformation. Behind these gardens lurks the inescapable pull of the *Georgics*, the *un*garden garden poem. And in this sense, there is an affinity with *Life & Times of Michael K*. For although K is a gardener, the novel is taken up with K's journey and his alienation. Neither subject nor setting, the garden in Coetzee's novel is an apparition of this universal human activity.

A nagging, persistent idea of the garden blooms throughout the novel, in its dense descriptions of war-torn South Africa and in its rich allegories that make K and his experiences symbolic of the brutality, starvation, and humiliation of apartheid. When the guerillas come to the farm, K does not join their forces. Instead, he hides,

> because enough men had gone off to war saying the time for gardening was when the war was over; whereas there must be men to stay behind and keep gardening alive, or at least the idea of gardening; because once that cord was broken, the earth would grow hard and forget her children (p. 109).

For Gordimer, the idea of the garden expresses the relationship that humans have with the earth, and what happens when humans not only destroy each other (as the whites and blacks in South Africa), but when they scorch, pollute, neglect and 'charge with radioactivity' the 'dirt beneath our feet' (1998, 143). Attridge rejects the notion that Coetzee 'celebrates or advocates ecological sensitivity' and instead argues that K's relation to the earth and to cultivation 'implies a resistance to modernity's drive to exploit natural resources'; and yet, for Attridge, this resistance never gains moral substance (2004, 53). The idea of the garden is just that: an idea, nothing more. It is, however, a powerful enough idea to form the single, albeit tenuous, bond that links K, the ultimate social outcast, to the rest of humanity (Heider 1993, 87).

When K is detained in the camp, the medical officer attempts to engage him in conversation. But K resists. As Augustine routinely engaged in conversation before his conversion, here K's refusal to converse thwarts any possibility for conversion or change. The medical officer tries by asking K what is in the packet he his holding, and K shows him dried pumpkin seeds. 'I was quite affected' says the officer, who then encourages K to 'go back to your gardening when the war is over ... It would be nice to see market gardening carried out in the peninsula again' (p. 135). But when K refuses to eat or to communicate, sending the officer into his imagined tirade, the garden loses its charm:

> Let me tell you the meaning of the sacred and alluring garden that blooms in the heart of the desert and produces the food of life. The garden for which you are presently heading is nowhere and everywhere except in the camps (p. 166).

Although reticent with the officer, K can be quite coherent in his thoughts. So he wins the last word over the medical officer, just four pages from the end of the novel:

> ... the truth is that I have been a gardener, first for the Council, later for myself, and gardeners spend their time with their noses to the ground.
> K tossed restlessly on the cardboard. It excited him, he found, to say, recklessly, *the truth, the truth about me. 'I am a gardener,'* he said again, aloud. (pp. 181-2, emphasis original).

113

Yet the narrator gets the last word over K: 'On the other hand, was it not strange for a gardener to be sleeping in a closet within sound of the beating of the waves of the sea?' (p. 182). How much more alienated could K be, than to assert his existence as a gardener, only to have this self-definition destroyed by the conditions of his survival? The idea of the garden, the connection with the soil and the connection that binds together an agricultural society, is good. In theory, K is a gardener. But in practice, deprived of property and peace, K's existence as a gardener will never be realized.

Before concluding, I would like to trace one more thread of interpretation by considering *Life & Times of Michael K* as a work of apartheid literature that engages in a perplexing moral dilemma. When K refuses to live in the farmhouse, choosing instead to live outdoors, Gordimer believes that he expresses in the starkest of terms the most pressing aspect of political debate about the future of South Africa under black majority rule: 'whether or not it should take over what has been the white South African version of the capitalist system' (Gordimer 1998, 142). This is the condition of colonial society: as the colonizer subjects the native, so the native rejects the colonizer. The problem is compounded, however, by an equally profound dependency. The colonizer depends on the native, not only for his social and material privilege, but also for his sense of moral superiority, and so finally for his identity. The native admires the technological and economic advances that the colonizer brings, but at the same time hates the system of oppression that conveys material prosperity (Jan-Mohamed 1983, 4). K longs for a place to live in peace, a place to garden. The only way he can achieve this is to move onto a farm that was owned, and is deserted, by whites. K's rejection of the farm buildings symbolizes a rejection of the apparatus of white domination. Ironically, such a rejection also denies K a permanent garden.

What could Augustine's garden in Milan and Coetzee's idea of the garden in *Life & Times of Michael K* possibly have in common? Indeed, more than you may think. Let us start with the similarities between authors. From Carthage to Cape Town, Augustine and Coetzee dwell on the extremes of the African continent. Both belong to multi-racial, polyglot worlds. Both were educated and employed abroad before returning to their native continent. Both are of European, not African stock. Both are controversial, prolific, and well-known authors in their

114

own times. In the works of both, the classics find a place (the main character in Coetzee's *Age of Iron,* for example, is a retired classics professor). Both live long enough to see the political systems (Roman rule and apartheid) under which they lived much of their lives crumble.

Furthermore, the *Confessions* and the *Life & Times of Michael K* both attempt to translate the random, disparate elements of lived experience – of life – into the form of a story (see Dovey 1988, 271). The very title of Coetzee's novel brings forward the central aspects of Augustine's autobiographical endeavour; life consists of the passing of time, yet the constraints of time complicate the ability to narrate life and indeed force the composition of order out of chaos. Augustine devotes an entire book of the *Confessions* to a meditation on time; Coetzee's novel, too, is marked by repeated references to time (Dovey 1988, 281). Both works strive to create the illusion of temporal sequence.

In both the *Confessions* and *Life & Times of Michael K*, the mother plays a central role, even if by her absence. Monica occupies a fair portion of the *Confessions* and may be considered the only other character in the autobiography of any substance. Her desire for Augustine's conversion compels the narrative, and her death threatens to bring the narrative to a premature conclusion. K's mother, Anna K, with her desire to return to the Karoo initiates the action of the novel. Instead of bringing the novel to a close, her death redirects the course of the novel and her burial gives K purpose.

Mothers and gardens both manifest generative, fertile reproduction. If sterile witches (like Canidia) and whores (like Messalina) do not belong in the garden, then mothers like Monica and Anna K do belong. Indeed, they are the catalysts that bring the garden into being. And yet, although they are necessary, they also need to be absent. They need to fade into the background, they need, in fact, to die, so that their sons' stories can move forward. As if to illustrate this need, Coetzee takes his mother as the subject of his brief and somewhat puzzling (or perhaps humorous, and at the least, entertaining) acceptance speech for the Nobel Prize in Literature – his mother, a compelling, yet absent, force:

My mother would have been bursting with pride. My son the Nobel Prize winner. And for whom, anyway, do we do the things that lead to Nobel Prizes if not for our mothers?

115

'Mommy, Mommy, I won a prize!'

'That's wonderful, my dear. Now eat your carrots before they get cold.'

Why must our mothers be ninety-nine and long in the grave before we can come running home with the prize that will make up for all the trouble we have been to them? (2004, 22)

It would not be difficult to imagine Augustine asking the same kind of question, and feeling the same kind of regret, that his mother could not be present for his achievements.

As a further point of comparison, both Augustine and Coetzee rely heavily on allegory. Braund succinctly defines allegory as 'a trope in which a second meaning is to be read beneath and concurrent with the surface story' (2002, 225), and Feeney traces its origins and use in classical literature (1991, 5-56). Building upon the terms of allegory evolved by Alexandrian Greek schools, Christian thinkers interpreted the Word of God and practised biblical exegesis; according to Brown, Augustine went one step further and 'produced a singularly comprehensive explanation of why allegory should have been necessary in the first place' (2000, 258). There is no doubt that Coetzee deploys allegory in his novel of the gardener; for example, the enigmatic main character, the avoidance of specificity when referring to the civil war or its partisans, and the distance from time and place invite the reader to understand these terms as having meaning beyond the literal so as to describe, without naming, the experience of apartheid and civil war in South Africa (see Gordimer 1998, 141). Attridge (2004, 34) points out that in *Life & Times of Michael K*, Coetzee takes allegory to new heights of that characteristic self-reference we have already witnessed as a defining feature of the novel, when the medical officer says, 'Your stay in the camp was merely an allegory, if you know that word. It was an allegory – speaking at the highest level – of how scandalously, how outrageously a meaning can take up residence in a system without becoming a term in it' (p. 166; see also Marais 2001, 115).

But at this point the similarities evaporate and we must tally the differences. According to Attridge, because of the repeated use of 'perhaps', and the way major themes are embedded, nearly hidden, in characters' thoughts and not made manifest in their actions, Coetzee invites the reader to resist allegorical interpretation. Allegory, by

assigning a correspondence between symbol and meaning, seals interpretation; when one resists allegory, then meanings are left open,
possibilities extended. Attridge neatly summarizes the difference between an allegorical reading and a resistance to allegory, a difference
manifested in Augustine's and Coetzee's varied uses of the trope:
'Allegory announces a moral code, literature invites an ethical response' (Attridge 2004, 64).

If Coetzee invites resistance to allegory and so an ethical response,
where Augustine insists on allegory and thereby announces a moral
code, so too they part company in their formulations of the central
philosophical and religious notion of 'calling'. Augustine, as we have
seen, positions himself in the tradition of the calling of Moses by God.
K, on the other hand, is relieved that he is *not* called: 'I am one of the
fortunate ones who escape being called' (p. 104; see Attridge 2004, 56).
For some critics, it is difficult to believe that this illiterate, impover-
ished outcast is capable of recognizing that he has not been called, let
alone capable of articulating this exclusion in such eloquent terms.
But could it not be the case that K's feebleness renders him that much
the more credible a witness of apartheid? The dissonance between K's
base social status and his eloquence in fact sustains the entire novel,
giving it an edge that cuts to the quick.

In the end, I set Augustine and Coetzee side by side not for their
similarities, but to throw into sharp relief the clearest of their differences. The *Confessions*, with Augustine's conversion in the garden in
Milan, is essentially a story of Christian redemption. And redemption
– etymologically the act of buying back or reclaiming by purchase –
activates a metaphor of economy. Consider how many times in the
Confessions, a work that is in the main a spiritual meditation,
Augustine openly talks about money. For example, he plainly states
his father's meagre earnings (2.3.5), in contrast to the wealth of his
patron Romanianus, a well-to-do citizen of Thagaste who took
Augustine under his wing (6.14). Throughout his career as a teacher,
Augustine is motivated by a need (and even a desire) to earn greater
profits (4.2, 5.8, 5.13, 6.6). Only after his conversion does he lose his
ambition to make money (9.2). Even in his description of sublime
divinity, he resorts to a metaphor of economy: 'You are never in need
and still you rejoice in profit, you are never greedy but still you collect
interest' (1.4.4).

117

His willingness to refer to income contrasts vividly with the usual Roman reticence on the subject. For example, the moral condemnation of turning profit, so strenuously voiced by Cato in the preface to his *On Agriculture*, contrasts with what we are told by Plutarch of Cato's own practice of earning wealth (Plutarch, *Life of Cato* 21.5). One thing is certain: The contradictions between the theory and practice of wealth left the Romans in a deep moral predicament. Augustine's frank statements about his financial situation may derive from the radically different structures of the pagan and Christian social systems and world views. Repeated references to personal assets keep the narrative grounded in a materiality and set the scene for the ultimate purchase: the redemption of his soul.

Redemption, 'buying back,' is an economic force of both religion and interpretation, and here I am indebted to the remarks of Martindale (1993, 101-7). As there is a price to be paid in belief, so there is a price to be paid in reading. The redemptive power of the *Confessions* lies in the fact that by reading, Augustine comes to belief. He recounts his readings of Vergil's *Aeneid* (1.13), Homer (1.14), Cicero's influential *Hortensius* (3.4), Aristotle's *Ten Categories* (4.16). 'I read and understood by myself all the books that I could find on the so-called liberal arts' (4.16); 'I had read a great many scientific books which were still alive in my memory' (5.3). After reading the neo-Platonists (7.9) and the letters of Paul (7.21), he finally arrives at scripture. 'Take, *read*; take, *read*' (8.12.29): these are the words that lead him to redemption. As he buys into text after text, so he reclaims his belief system. Similarly, however, as Augustine constructs and reconstructs his belief system in the *Confessions*, so he constructs and reconstructs interpretations, not only of the texts that bring him to conversion, but the very text that he writes. In doing so, he buys back his beloved reader from the market place in which he himself was once lost. If conversation leads to conversion, reading leads to redemption. None of this happens, though, unless one is ready – that is, unless one has read.

By contrast, according to Durrant, 'Coetzee's narratives rigorously resist the teleology of redemption' (2004, 49). *Life & Times of Michael K* would appear to be unexceptional in this regard. My sense, however, is that Coetzee seeks, not to deny redemption, but to secularize it, by divorcing its interpretive dimension from the religious, and replacing that religious dimension (that Augustinian moral code) with an ethical response. The reader may not be redeemed by the story of K, but he will have spent something on the effort.

Perhaps this is what fascinates me most about the powerful image of the garden, this token in the economy of representation, that one thing, the garden, can so prosperously and so swiftly settle the debts of such radically different authorial ledgers: 'Here is the garden poem: payment in full,' says Columella (*On Agriculture* 10, Preface 1; above p. 31). On the other hand, Finlay regards gardens as perpetually insolvent: gardens are always for *next* year. If a metaphor of economy reminds us of the materiality – the time and space – of the garden, it also demands ethical responsibility (Coetzee 1984, 6). In the end, the search for the garden in the Roman literary imagination begins with just two simple questions: How much can an author afford to spend on a garden? And how much does it cost the reader to ask?

The Invention of Gardens

Gardens should not scruple to provide a setting in
which pigeons can appear as doves.

Ian Hamilton Finlay

I

The garden, with its clearly defined boundary, invites transgression
that yields transformation. The undeniable beauty of the garden
induces a trance-like reverie from which the author, caught up in
describing the garden's pleasures, may recall himself back to the task
at hand. To be sure, all authors labour under the anxiety of representation, the fear that their narratives will fall short of the reality
they attempt to portray; literature about gardens likewise betrays this
anxiety. Finally, in as much as this is a study of border-crossing, it is
by default a study of the representations of women and the gendered
discourse that portrays women as transgressive figures.

A logical place to begin a study of the garden in the Roman literary
imagination would have been with Cato's treatise *On Agriculture*. It
immediately became the authority for the prose works of Varro,
Columella, Pliny, and even for Vergil's hexameter *Georgics*. However,
it is important to bear in mind that Cato's *On Agriculture* was written
on the eve of the final destruction of Carthage and the sack of Corinth
in the fateful year 146 BCE. Cato writes in response to the revolutionary practices of investment farming and the rise of *latifundia*.
Although never formally defined, *latifundium* was originally a neutral
term for a large estate; the word took on a sense of moral disapproval
of the degeneracy associated with the chain gangs and debt-bondsmen
who were employed on such large estates. In the Roman way of
thinking, an estate that was too large for the owner to manage himself
was morally suspect. Furthermore, farming was traditionally the
occupation of a peasant citizen who, if needed, left his farm to serve in

the army. The shift in the composition of the army resulted in a displacement of the role of the farmer as well. Thus, the dominant mood of Cato's *On Agriculture* is the moral imperative. As if to counter the dubious moral position of the *latifundia*, Cato's manual never betrays a doubt as to how such an estate should be run. It is important to remember that the Roman agricultural writing that follows in the tradition of Cato inherently imports this moralizing tone. Over the next two hundred years, Varro, Columella, and Pliny the Elder refer to Cato as if he were the authority, even when they challenge him on a particular point (on Columella's neutral use of Cato, see Baldwin 1963, 787). Later writers gloss the fact that Cato was writing in response to a large-scale economic revolution in Roman society. Furthermore, Reay has demonstrated the way that Cato's *On Agriculture* manifests tensions between continuity and change, individual and society. The treatise is a performance of a 'corporate, aristocratic identity', while at the same time it conveys Cato's individual expression of this phenomenon (Reay 2005). This aristocratic self-fashioning, seen as a response to the crisis produced by rapid geopolitical expansion in the post-Hannibalic era, further distinguishes Roman agricultural writing from its Greek counterpart.

In following Cato, Columella partakes in this distinctly Roman dialogue of morals. Sometimes Cato is the authority, for example, 'Cato believed that in inspecting farm land the two most important considerations were climate and productivity of the location' (*On Agriculture* 1.3.1; see also 1.3.5, 1.4.1, 1.4.8), or 'The overseer, as Cato says, should not be a gadabout' (1.8.7). Sometimes, however, he is a source of controversy (e.g., 3.3.2, 3.9.3, 4.11.1). By Columella's time, Cato was regarded as the founder of Roman agricultural writing: 'Now let us recall Marcus Cato the Censor, who first undertook to write about it in Latin' (1.1.12). Cato's Roman readers seem to overlook the radical nature of Cato's writing, thereby adopting his authority on farming without question.

In order to escape from the shadow of this particularly Catonian moralizing discourse, I chose instead to look at gardens in out-of-the-way places. By looking at representations of gardens in an agricultural treatise, a satire, an annalistic history, and an autobiography, we have been able to discern the garden in a literary imagination that belonged to a Roman mentality. Along the way, I have suggested that some

122

modern works of literature also exhibit some characteristics of garden literature. The Japanese garden in Forché's lyric poem and the pumpkin garden in Coetzee's *Life & Times of Michael K* are powerful political images. However, such comparisons run the risk of attenuating the force of my argument about ancient Roman literature. Horace's poem about a farting statue can hardly hold a candle to the stark realities of apartheid portrayed by Coetzee. Tacitus' convoluted sensationalism (no matter how much he disavows it) pales in comparison to Forché's candid confrontation with nuclear holocaust. So, are these classics relevant only if they can be proven to be the foundation for modern literature (in the same way, for example, one cannot understand Joyce's *Ulysses* without reading Homer)? Is it the case that one cannot fully appreciate the garden imagery in Forché or Coetzee without understanding the garden in the Roman literary imagination?

Of course not. Rather, I hope to have shown that the garden has a powerful hold over the imagination across genres, across eras, and that authors and readers should be keenly aware of this seductive power. If the chief feature of gardens is the clearly defined boundary, then the chief feature of garden literature is its seductive ability to lead author and reader to transgress generic decorum and to generate a transformation in those who read and write about them. This book is meant to put a brake on interpretations of garden literature that wax rhapsodic on themes such as regeneration, growth, life, timeless beauty, and its constant companion, truth. You may think I am spoiling fun, but I believe I am insisting on a certain degree of responsibility. I would not and do not deny that I have also fallen victim to the garden's potential to rob me of my senses. This book as much as any other garden book (or book about gardens, or representations of gardens) lives up to its generic expectations; however, at least I know where I have over-interpreted, under-theorized, and hyper-rhetoricized.

II

The British playwright Stoppard and his critically acclaimed play *Arcadia* make a fitting conclusion to this book for several reasons. First of all, drama is not a particularly Roman genre. While technical garden writing, satire, annalistic history, and autobiography are uniquely Roman genres, Roman drama, on the other hand, owed a great deal of its form and content to the Greek playwrights. Our sources are extremely limited; although the Romans produced hundreds of plays, only a handful from the comic playwrights Plautus and Terence survive from the early second century BCE, and nothing further until the first century CE with the tragedies of Seneca the Younger. Yet, in spite of the paucity of sources, it is possible to discern something of the Roman attitudes toward drama. The Romans had a peculiar distrust of, and distaste for, actors and their profession. The public display of one's body ran counter to the Roman value of *dignitas*, or personal dignity. Public performances had the potential to stir up the crowds and incite public disorder. Theatre falls prey to the xenophobic discourse of Republican writers who attribute theatrical performances in Rome to the corrupting influence, pernicious idleness, and perverse sexuality of foreigners. Actors were among the most legally restricted professionals in ancient Rome, sharing a social status comparable to gladiators and prostitutes. They suffered no protection from corporal punishment; they could not lodge accusations in court; they could not serve as a magistrate or a soldier in the army, and they were not counted as members of tribal assemblies (see Edwards 1997 on the status of actors in Rome). Of course, such social and legal measures reinforced a cycle of marginalization; with no privileges to lose, actors had no reason to adhere to standards of civic behaviour. Drama, therefore, is about as un-Roman a genre as can be, and so it makes a good 'control' in our experiment, a good way to measure what we have said about *Roman* genres against an un-Roman genre. It is possible that the Romans *did* have a particular way of thinking about gardens and that it is closely tied to their literary expressions and the literary forms that they developed.

Secondly, theatre is an ephemeral art-form, and so like gardens, it is designed to live and breathe. A performance belongs to the moment and can never be replicated. Likewise, a garden changes from season to season, and even day to day, so that one never really experiences the same garden twice. Thus, both the theatre and the garden are kinetic evolutions. In many ways, then, this book is a fitting companion to Rehm's recent contribution to this Classical Inter/Faces series, in which he speculates on the inextricable relationship between performance and temporality.

124

5. The Invention of Gardens

Thirdly, the film productions of *Rosencrantz and Guildenstern are Dead* (1991) and *Shakespeare in Love* (1999) earned Stoppard wide recognition in popular culture. The former was Stoppard's first critical success. In 1967 the National Theatre produced *Rosencrantz and Guildenstern are Dead*, making Stoppard at twenty-nine years of age the youngest playwright to have a play performed in that prestigious venue. Furthermore, the play was the first to transfer from the National Theatre to New York, where after 421 performances it won a Tony Award for best play in 1968. In 1991, the film version was released, demonstrating the ability for Stoppard's genius to retain its brilliance in another medium. *Shakespeare in Love* won three Golden Globe awards, including best screenplay, and seven Academy Awards including best screenplay and best picture. Stoppard was knighted in 1997.

First produced in 1993, *Arcadia* is regarded by many as Stoppard's greatest play (Edwards 2001, 171). Delaney refers to '*Arcadia*, the stage play that may well be his masterpiece' (2001, 34). For Zinman, 'the greatness of *Arcadia*' derives from the intersection of difficult ideas and fully human characters (2001, 134). Although one critic called *Arcadia* 'the snob hit of the season' (Tinker in Nadel 2002, 445), most agreed that the play was 'the perfect marriage of ideas and high comedy' (Nightingale in Nadel 2002, 445). The popularity of *Arcadia* is easily measured by the retail sales of the script at the National Theatre; during its run, it exceeded all other plays in print, including the works of Shakespeare. According to Nadel, *Arcadia* sold 6,000 copies in the first three weeks. By 1995, *Arcadia* had played for 431 performances. In addition to box-office and print success, *Arcadia* enjoyed the critical acclaim of Stoppard's colleagues. The play was produced in Zurich, New York, San Francisco, Chicago, Prague, and Paris. The University of Pennsylvania, Berkeley's Mathematical Sciences Research Institute, and Stanford University devoted symposia to the play (Nadel 2002, 447, 450).

Stoppard seems to write plays in pairs that can be paired with plays of Shakespeare. Thus, the contiguity of *Shakespeare in Love* with *Romeo and Juliet* continues and in many ways completes the task of reworking Shakespeare begun in *Rosencrantz and Guildenstern are Dead*, whose other half, so to speak, is *Hamlet*. Similarly, the project of *Arcadia*, with its themes of Classicism versus Romanticism, finds a twin in *The Invention of Love*, first produced at the National Theatre

125

in 1997 (on twinning and doubling as a feature of Stoppard's work, see Doll 1993, 118; Delaney 2001). *Arcadia* and *The Invention of Love* share structural and thematic characteristics. For example, both plays meld two time periods into one plot. *Arcadia* shuttles between events in 1809-12 and 1989. *The Invention of Love* is a memory play in which the main character, AEH (A.E. Housman, aged seventy-seven), confronts and has a dialogue with Housman (A.E. Housman, aged from eighteen to twenty-six). In both plays, the sexuality of central characters is repressed, while certain peripheral characters engage in sexual excesses. In *Arcadia*, the plot is driven by the insatiable lust of Mrs Chater, who never appears on stage, while Thomasina's virginity in the past is echoed in Hannah's resolute abstinence in the present. In *The Invention of Love*, Housman's repressed homosexuality is foiled by Oscar Wilde's flamboyance. Even in their mechanics, the plays resemble each other. Both require especially large casts and are therefore expensive to produce. Both drew criticism for being overly intellectual and therefore inaccessible, *Arcadia* with its mathematics and chaos theory, and *The Invention of Love* with its classical philology and textual criticism.

The Invention of Love is a highly controversial play. While one critic hailed it as 'the most emotionally powerful and enthralling play of the year' (de Jongh in Nadel 2002, 512-13), another found it insufferable and stated that 'I would rather have spent the evening in a darkened cell. Standing in a corner, facing the wall' (Sexton in Nadel 2002, 513). Furthermore, the play sparked a caustic debate between critic and playwright in the *New York Review*, where a polemical review by classicist Daniel Mendelsohn prompted Stoppard, for the first time, to respond in defence.

For Mendelsohn, Stoppard's portrayal of Housman was one-sided, focusing solely on the irritable professor to the exclusion of the beloved poet. Mendelsohn furthermore objected to Stoppard's misuse of intellectual matter in the play (a similar criticism launched against *Arcadia*) and charged, 'For all their intellectual trimmings, Stoppard's plays are, ultimately, anti-intellectual' (Mendelsohn, August 2000, 63). In his reply, Stoppard asserted that Mendelsohn's 'Happy Housman is no more persuasive than the permanently miserable misanthrope he says is mine' (Stoppard, September 2000,103), to which Mendelsohn responded that the play's popularity derives from

126

Stoppard's ambivalence about people who pursue knowledge for its own sake (Mendelsohn, September 2000,104). Stoppard tried again to convince the critic in a second reply, to which Mendelsohn countered with equal sarcasm (October 2000, 64-5). The fact that both playwright and critic were compelled to compose two exchanges suggests to me that *The Invention of Love* conveys some important and disconcerting messages.

The Invention of Love grapples with, among other issues, the usefulness of classical scholarship. The central character is the notorious classical scholar and English poet A.E. Housman – another instance of Stoppard's doubling in a character with two facets (scholar/poet), two names (AEH/Housman), two ages (77/18-26), two occupations (clerk in patent office/classical philologist). The Latin poetry of Horace and Catullus is incorporated throughout the play, lending insight into the reception of the Roman literary imagination in the contemporary English-speaking world. The Latin and Greek languages challenged actors, audience, and even playwright, although Stoppard did study Latin. 'It's not gibberish to me,' he said in an interview, 'But I read it with cribs' (Gussow 1995, 85). Peter Jones, author of *Learn Latin*, assisted with pronunciation and scansion; David West, scholar of Latin poetry and translator of the *Aeneid*, with technical matters. In a way, *The Invention of Love* does for classics on the stage what Ridley Scott's academy award winning film *Gladiator* does for classics on the screen. Both succeed, to an extent, in arousing in general audiences an interest in the classics. One reviewer claimed that Stoppard's dialogue on classical poetry was filled with 'such passion, wit and verve, you feel like signing up for a classics course on the spot' (Gore-Langton in Nadel 2002, 512). Mendelsohn remarks, 'When I saw the play in March with a classicist friend of mine, we were amazed to see that the audience was rapt as Housman explained, in technical language that refused to condescend to the nonclassicist, how his emendation worked' (August 2000, 63). Finally, *The Invention of Love* is an exploration of homosexuality that – like the Classical Inter/Faces series itself – calls into question the ethics of the enterprise of interpretations of classical antiquity. Taken together, both *Arcadia* and *The Invention of Love* demonstrate the various ways Stoppard manipulates time and space to create – indeed, to invent – gardens on stage.

III

The broad comedy of *Arcadia*, with its seemingly endless round of star-crossed, mismatched, and unrequited lovers, unfolds like any good mystery whose every clue is presented at some point but whose solution is only accessible when at last everything is laid out on the table. In 1989, two scholars, Bernard Nightingale and Hannah Jarvis, come to Sidley Park, a country estate in Derbyshire, each in search of the answer to a specific question. He asks, did the famous British poet George Gordon, Lord Byron, kill a second-rate poet named Ezra Chater in a duel? She is in search of the identity of the hermit of Sidley Park. Bernard Nightingale is a vain and conceited professor who is convinced he has solved the riddle of the poet Lord Byron's sudden and heretofore unexplained departure from England in 1810, and without sufficient evidence, rushes recklessly to untenable conclusions. Hannah Jarvis, author of a recent best-selling novel, is determined to write a book about a hermit who lived in the garden at Sidley Park. Living in the present-day estate are the Coverly heirs Chloë and her brothers Valentine and Gus. The fifteen-year-old Gus is a silent 'genius' who falls in love with Hannah. Valentine is a mathematician who by using the game books of the estate tries to find the pattern underlying the changing grouse population. He provides much of the interpretation of mathematical principles at the core of the play. The virulent arguments between Valentine and Bernard also depict the battle between science and poetry, Enlightenment and Romanticism, thinking and feeling.

As Bernard and Hannah attempt to unravel the mysteries of the past, the past is laid before the audience. The play is set in two different time periods, but in the exact same place. The curtain opens to a room on the garden front of Sidley Park in April 1809. The only furnishings are a very large table with straight-backed chairs and a reading stand; the floor is bare. The entire play takes place in this room, with no set change whatsoever. Only the props belie the progress of the plot and the interface of the past (1809-12) with the present (1989). Each successive scene adds its vestiges to the table: books, an apple, a compass, letters, papers.

Thomasina Coverly, daughter of the lady of the manor, and her tutor Septimus Hodge are engaged in lessons. The play opens with a deliciously comic question: 'Septimus, what is carnal embrace?'

5. The Invention of Gardens

Thomasina overheard the butler say that one of the guests at Sidley Park, a Mrs Chater, was discovered in 'carnal embrace' in the gazebo. During the lesson, we learn the identity of Mrs Chater's paramour. Mr Chater challenges Septimus to a duel; the tutor skilfully talks himself out of the confrontation by suggesting that he will write a favourable review of Chater's latest poem, 'The Couch of Eros'. In gratitude, Chater inscribes the book of poetry to Septimus.

At this point, Lady Croom, mistress of the estate, enters the room with her brother Captain Brice and Mr Noakes, the landscape artist. She bemoans the proposed renovations to her garden, which would do away with her gazebo, the boat house, the Chinese bridge, and the shrubbery. Noakes has provided a sketch book with 'before' and 'after' views of the landscape. Lady Croom takes up the book:

> Your drawing is a very wonderful transformation. I would not have recognized my own garden but for your ingenious book – is it not? – look! Here is the Park as it appears to us now, and here it might be when Mr Noakes has done with it. Where there is the familiar pastoral refinement of an Englishman's garden, here is an eruption of gloomy forest and towering crag, of ruins where there was never a house, of water dashing against rocks where there was neither a spring nor a stone I could not throw the length of a cricket pitch. My hyacinth dell is become a haunt for hobgoblins, my Chinese bridge, which I am assured is superior to the one at Kew, and for all I know at Peking, is usurped by a fallen obelisk overgrown with briars – (*Arcadia*, pp. 11-12).

We have encountered such garden rhetoric before. First, the garden is a locus of incipient transformation, for, like the transformation of the Gardens of Maecenas from pauper's cemetery, the transformation has not yet been completed. As a result, in both *Arcadia* and *Satire* 1.8, the garden encompasses both 'then' and 'now.' Secondly, the garden's transformation is filtered through several layers of representation. The audience does not see Noakes' drawing but rather hears Lady Croom's ecphrastic description of the illustrated transformation. Finally, this passage demonstrates most clearly the way that, although transformed, a garden always retains some aspect of its earlier appearance that can be recognized. As the vestiges of the pauper's

129

cemetery could still be seen in the Gardens of Maecenas, as Shukkei-en reflects the layers of its reconstructed past, so Lady Croom can still recognize her garden at Sidley Park, in spite of the violent changes from an Italian classical countryside to a gloomy Gothic wilderness.

Whereas in Forché's poem, the atomic bomb brutally and purpose-fully destroyed the Japanese garden, in Stoppard's play, ruin and destruction are contrived affectations. The crag, the haunt, and the fallen obelisk overgrown with briars are not the result of the ravages of time but rather the conceited impositions of the gardener's hand on nature. Lady Croom objects to the Romantic reworking of Sidley Park, describing its classical perfection:

> But Sidley Park is already a picture, and a most amiable picture too. The slopes are green and gentle. The trees are companion-ably grouped at intervals that show them to advantage. The rill is a serpentine ribbon unwound from the lake peaceably con-tained by meadows on which the right amount of sheep are tastefully arranged – in short, it is nature as God intended (*Arcadia*, p. 12).

Lady Croom's preference is no less contrived than the renovator's vision, and both neatly summarize the shift in English garden styles, from Classical to Romantic. Sidley Park witnesses the transition from one era to the next, and the theme of the triumph of emotions over reason governs the rest of the play.

The second scene is set in the same room, 180 years later, in 1989. Bernard Nightingale has come to Sidley Park to meet Hannah Jarvis, author of a recent book on Byron, to see if she has any more informa-tion about the nineteenth-century Coverlys, and a certain Ezra Chater in particular. He has come into possession of Chater's 'The Couch of Eros', inscribed to Septimus Hodge, which was among Byron's posses-sions. Bernard constructs an elaborate hypothesis (which the audience learns by degrees is false), that Byron wrote scathing reviews of Chater's poems, Byron seduced Mrs Chater, Byron was challenged to a duel by the husband, and Byron killed Chater. The third scene returns to April 1809 where it is revealed that Septimus in fact reviewed Chater's poems and reluctantly loaned his copy of Chater's 'The Couch of Eros' to his friend Byron.

5. The Invention of Gardens

In scene four, Valentine tries to explain to Hannah the mathematics that Thomasina left in her notebook. Falling as it does in the middle of the play, this scene is crucial to the audience's understanding of the chaos theory that informs so much of the play's substance. In scene five, Bernard delivers a practice run of his lecture on his discoveries about Byron before an appreciative Chloë; however, Valentine and Hannah cannot help but interrupt Bernard with objections to his conjectures. Nevertheless, Bernard rushes to London to deliver his paper and stake his scholarly claim.

Septimus' derisive review of Chater's first poem, 'The Maid of Turkey', in which he wrote 'he would not give it to his dog for dinner were it covered in bread sauce and stuffed with chestnuts' (p. 8), has as its counterpart Bernard's review of Hannah's book, of which we are likewise given only a glimpse: 'Byron the spoilt child promoted beyond his gifts by the spirit of the age! And Caroline the closet intellectual shafted by a male society!' (p. 60). Like Noakes' drawings of the gardens, Chater's poem and Hannah's book are ecphrases; they are not actualized on stage but described to the audience by a third party. In these ways, *Arcadia* is a lens through which these works are viewed, like the theodolite on the table, used to view the landscape. Stoppard also calls attention to the review as a more tangible, more lasting incarnation of a work. Chater's poem and Hannah's book exist in *Arcadia* only to the extent that they are *un*favourably reviewed. The audience is given only the critic's disapproving words. I suggest that Stoppard, anticipating the reviews that will follow the production of *Arcadia*, reminds the audience in a metatheatrical move of the rules of critical discourse in Bernard's line, 'I will be taking questions at the end. Constructive comments will be welcome' (p. 55). The trouble for Bernard is, of course, that the critics do not wait until the end. The characters lose patience with each other and the scene devolves from heated argument to *ad hominem* attack, written as if by a veteran of the review wars.

Scene six reveals to the audience the actual course of events as they happened on the estate 'then'. On the morning of 10 April, Septimus woke at 5 am to meet Mr Chater in the garden for the duel. Septimus returned to the house with only a rabbit, for Mr Chater did not show. He learns from the butler that Captain Brice (who had brought the Chaters to his sister's estate) had left Sidley Park with the couple,

131

driven off by his sister Lady Croom, because of Mrs Chater's overt sexual indiscretions. Lord Byron had also left the estate, taking Septimus' book with him.

Lady Croom then enters the school room, and Septimus' affections for her are revealed. He confesses to his 'carnal embrace' with Mrs Chater in the gazebo but explains that she was only a hollow substitute for the lover he really desired, and in Lady Croom's absence he was driven to such a desperate measure. As for Chater's disappearance from the literary record (the mystery that set Bernard on his scholarly chase), Chater was not killed in a duel. Rather, he followed Brice to the Indies to practise botany; there he was bitten by a monkey and died within the year. Brice was free to marry Mrs Chater, with whom he had been having an affair all along.

In scene seven, the past and present, 'then' and 'now', coalesce; two pairs of characters (Septimus and Thomasina, Bernard and Hannah) occupy the stage and dialogue simultaneously. Bernard has become famous for his 'discovery' of the poet Chater and his role in the mysterious departure of Byron. He has discovered two reviews of Chater's poetry written by Byron, hitherto unknown. He has explained the mysterious death of this otherwise unknown poet Chater: he was killed by Byron in a duel. Headlines read 'Even in Arcadia – Sex, Literature and Death at Sidley Park', and 'Byron Fought Fatal Duel, Says Don', and 'Bonking Byron Shot Poet' (pp. 73, 74). Bernard, however, learns the truth from the evidence finally uncovered by Hannah from Lady Croom's garden book. The harsh language of the denouement is especially dramatic:

Bernard: Oh, no – no –
Hannah: I'm sorry, Bernard.
Bernard: Fucked by a dahlia! Do you think? Is it open and shut? Am I fucked? What does it really amount to? When all's said and done? Am I fucked? What do *you* think, Valentine? Tell me the truth.
Valentine: You're fucked.
Bernard: Oh God! Does it mean that?
Hannah: Yes, Bernard, it does .... It means that Ezra Chater of the Sidley Park connection is the same Chater who described a

dwarf dahlia in Martinique in 1810 and died there, of a monkey
bite. (pp. 88-9, emphasis original)

How ironic: a metaphorical 'fuck' by a dahlia unravels the mysteries
of Sidley Park, that were indeed created by so much sexual intercourse. And it is ironic that Hannah should present Bernard with the
potent dahlia. He failed in his attempts to seduce and overpower her,
but she succeeds in emasculating him with her discovery. Bernard is
confronted by the potent fertility of the garden, in which the dahlia
becomes a sort of Priapus, capable of driving out intruders with false
notions. Then, one last time, the notion of the review is reprised.
Hannah promises to write an article correcting Bernard: 'The day
after tomorrow. A letter in *The Times*.' This time, now that she has the
upper hand, *she* reminds *him* of the rules of discourse: 'It'll be very
short, very dry, absolutely gloat-free ... dignified congratulations to a
colleague, in the language of scholars' (p. 90). Stoppard points to the
regulation of speech on two levels, in art and in criticism, in literature
and in review. As the play follows a prescribed form, so too the review
must follow certain prescriptions so as to maintain its authority. The
critic cannot simply rave. As the play is indebted to the critic, so
criticism too has its rules.

Like the aged Housman (AEH) in *The Invention of Love* in search
of 'a small victory over ignorance and error, a scrap of knowledge to
add to our stock' (*Invention of Love* p. 38), so Bernard believes the only
contribution to knowledge is an empirical discovery. He learns, too
late, that he would have been much better off abandoning empiricist
history and opting for hermeneutics. This is the dichotomy that drives
a wedge in modern classical scholarship and becomes, as we shall see,
the cornerstone of *The Invention of Love*, where Housman is the last
great champion of the science of textual criticism before the dawn of a
new era of scholars who take as their starting question not the 'what'
but the 'why', and to my mind, obviously, go a step further toward
understanding the past, even if only by inches.

Bernard departs, and Hannah and Valentine thus occupy the stage,
each engaged in their own research; Valentine makes one last attempt
to explain Thomasina's notebooks to Hannah. In the meantime,
Thomasina and Septimus also occupy the stage. It is 1812, the eve of
Thomasina's seventeenth birthday, and she attempts one last time to

133

seduce Septimus. She kisses him full on the mouth and begs him to teach her to waltz. He submits, and as they dance on stage, so Hannah relents to dancing with Gus, for it is the evening of the annual district gala. The play ends as past and present are inextricably woven together in dance.

In the final dialogue between Thomasina and Septimus, we are given one last metatheatrical moment, a hint of authorial self-awareness, when Stoppard breaks the fourth wall and speaks, in a way, to the audience. As Thomasina and Septimus speak to each other, so Valentine and Hannah also carry on a conversation. The speakers and addressees of the lines are easy enough to discern, until Valentine says, 'She didn't have the maths, not remotely. She saw what things meant, way ahead, like seeing a picture.' Septimus' reply to Thomasina, however, reads like a reply to Valentine's observation: 'This is not science, this is story telling' (*Arcadia*, p. 93). This bit of metatheatre reminds the audience that the purpose of the play is not to expound on chaos theory or the second law of thermodynamics, but rather to narrate a story, even if that story does not live up to the reality it attempts to portray. There lurks behind such a statement an anxiety of representation. Yet such procataleptic refutation effectively disarms criticism.

In the end, the garden play *Arcadia* is not characterized by the disparity in conceptual analysis in the same way that in *On Agriculture* 10 and *Satire* 1.8, Columella and Horace recall themselves from the seductive powers of the garden. On the contrary, it is as if Stoppard is very aware and never allows himself to slip into the grasp of the garden. When Bernard first meets Hannah, she is removing her muddy shoes because she has 'been in the ha-ha, very squelchy' (p. 20). But Bernard corrects her pronunciation, 'Ha-*hah*!' and explains:

A theory of mine. Ha-hah, not ha-ha. If you were strolling down the garden and all of a sudden the ground gave way at your feet, you're not going to go, 'ha-ha', you're going to jump back and go 'ha-hah!', or more probably, 'Bloody 'ell!'

Bernard is not ever about to step into a ha-ha, and so he can offer only a theory. In the same way, *Arcadia* resists stepping into the rhetoric of the garden. The consistently crisp dialogue eschews flowery descriptions; the closest approximation is Lady Croom's lament over the destruction of her beautiful classical garden, itself a parody.

Nor does Stoppard offer clear-cut instances of authorial self-awareness, in the way that Tacitus and Augustine punctuate their narratives with statements in the first person. In *Arcadia*, Stoppard is not revealed, even though there are metatheatrical moments when the text qua performance reveals its status as a written/performed object. It is fascinating to note that these instances point to the relationship of the playwright to the critic, and in this sense *Arcadia* partakes in the anxiety of representation. Stoppard is aware that some people may not understand all that he is trying to convey in his play, and that he may not be able to construct a play that conveys his every intention. His task is formidable and ambitious: to write a murder mystery about chaos theory, Newton's second law of thermodynamics, eighteenth-century garden history, academia, lust, and love. In the midst of all of this, however, he manages to slip the critic a few guidelines for judging his efforts along the way. If Stoppard earns hard-won success, perhaps that is because, to a certain degree, he also wills it.

IV

In Horace's *Satire* 1.8, the garden (a former cemetery) can encompass both 'then' and 'now.' We should consider carefully the implications of the way the two different temporal settings of *Arcadia* ('then' and 'now,' 1809-12 and 1989) share the same physical stage. As I mentioned in the Introduction, space has four social components: accessibility, appropriation, domination, and production. It would seem that by forcing two different eras to share the same space, Stoppard is attempting to overcome some of these socially enforced limitations. The same space is accessible to both eras. Neither era completely appropriates nor dominates the space. By sharing the space, the two time periods actually merge to produce a third space that exists neither in 1809 nor in 1989, but in the present of the actual, live theatrical performance.

The garden at Sidley Park, however, the 'Arcadia' of the play's title, is not at all released from Harvey's four constraints of space. First, Sidley Park is accessible only to the nobles who dwell there and to their privileged guests. In fact, those who do not behave suitably are ejected from the garden, namely the wanton Mrs Chater, her cuckold husband, and Captain Brice, the one responsible for their presence at the manor in the first place. Even in 1989, Bernard is eventually dismissed from Sidley Park after he is caught attempting to seduce Chloë in the cottage. Sidley Park is defined by its restricted access. Second, Sidley Park is most certainly open to appropriation. In 1809, the garden is completely transformed by the gardener, Richard Noakes. He obliterated the Classical eighteenth-century pastoral landscaping and replaced it with gloomy and Romantic features: crags, waterfalls, thickets, artificial ruins, and a hermitage. The garden is a contested space in which the ideals of Classicism are sacrificed to the progress of Romanticism. Third, many characters in the play attempt to dominate the landscape and to use their knowledge of the landscape to dominate other characters in the play. Thus it is that Bernard's theory is unravelled by the dahlia; the dahlia planted in the garden and its record in the garden book provide the key to unlock the entire plot. Finally, in terms of production, Stoppard's radical use of space calls into question the notion that there is a time and a place for everything, for in his theatrical production, there are two times for one place; one place can be occupied by two (indeed three) separate times.

Stoppard deftly juggles three time periods (1809, 1989, and the present moment of the production) before an audience that is continually asked to judge the value of each individual era. The past (1809) is shown to be as morally corrupt, if not more morally corrupt, than the present. However, characters in the past were capable of making profound scientific discoveries, and in that sense, the past measures up to, and in a sense exceeds the present. Stoppard also pits cyclical time against teleological time. The play begins and ends with teasing allusions to sexual attraction between Septimus and Thomasina. In the final scene, the two eras are intertwined in a dance; the Coverlys of 1989 are holding an annual gala; Septimus and Thomasina waltz on the same stage as Hannah and Gus. It seems as if time turns back on itself. However, the entire play is driven by Thomasina's innocent observation that 'When you stir your rice pudding, Septimus, the spoonful of jam spreads itself round making red trails like the picture of a meteor in my astronomical atlas. But if you stir backward, the jam will not come together again …. You cannot stir things apart' (pp. 4-5).

136

Thus, the sequence of events in 1809 follows in order and leads the audience to understand what happened at Sidley Park; the way these events occurred directly impacts the characters in 1989. Byron did not kill Chater, and so Bernard must be led to the same conclusion, eventually, 180 years later. As 'you cannot stir things apart', so you cannot undo the past. Part of the captivating charm of *Arcadia* is Stoppard's ability to challenge the constraints of time and space by the simultaneity of action on the stage and by the contiguity of space across decades.

One of the reasons *Arcadia* is capable of sustaining this collision of time and space ideologies is because it takes place in a room on the edge of a garden. In *Arcadia*, the garden's capacity for conflicting time and space is brilliantly portrayed. For a while, Stoppard succeeds in breaking the boundaries of time and space. Perhaps this is what gives the end of the play its most poignant mood. The audience mourns not the imminent, untimely death of the barely seventeen-year-old Thomasina, not the way Hannah substitutes the pursuit of knowledge for passion (in a way that anticipates Housman in *The Invention of Love*), but the realization that this freedom from the constraints of time and space is itself coming to an end. Perhaps what the audience mourns most of all is the walk to the parking lot. Perhaps this is why Plato so objected to the poets; what gives Stoppard the right to disappoint us so?

V

Some critics have made the charge that Stoppard 'can't do women' (Hunter 2000, 233). There are no female characters in *Rosencrantz and Guildenstern Are Dead*. In *Jumpers* (1972), both women are seen naked, objects of the male gaze. In *Travesties* (1974), one woman is required to perform an erotic dance, another to read aloud a suggestive poem; both are personal assistants to men. Such female characters are admitted only in service 'to inter-male discourses about reality, morality, art and political power' (Hunter 2000, 234). When it comes to women, however, Stoppard does make some progress in *Arcadia*. In a cast of thirteen characters, four are women: Thomasina and Lady Croom, Hannah Jarvis and Chloë Coverly. Hunter hails Hannah as a 'shrewd anchor-figure,' and Thomasina as a 'marvellous

137

– and respectful – study of female adolescence' (Hunter 2000, 234). The progress, however, is meagre, and Hunter's interpretation of the specific attributes of only two specific characters is valid only to a certain extent. Overall, I do not believe that women are portrayed favourably in *Arcadia*.

First of all, the catalyst for most of the plot in 1809 is Mrs Chater, who never appears on stage. The insatiable Mrs Chater, whom Septimus describes in the most degrading of terms: 'Her chief renown is for a readiness that keeps her in a state of tropical humidity as would grow orchids in her drawers in January' (*Arcadia*, p. 7). As Noakes and Lady Croom argue over the reconstruction of the garden, Septimus misunderstands their references to the gazebo, the boat-house, the Chinese bridge and the shrubbery. He ingenuously admits to having had sex with Mrs Chater in the gazebo ('I regret the gazebo, I sincerely regret the gazebo,' p. 10) and the boat-house, but denies having had sex with her on the Chinese Bridge or in the shrubbery. Mrs Chater is also discovered in Lord Byron's room (p. 70). Once dismissed from Sidley Park, she accompanies Captain Brice to the Indies to play 'mistress of the Captain's quarters' (p. 71).

Hannah, the clear-headed 'anchor-figure' is repressed and frigid. She denies Chloë's observation that 'there was a lot of sexual energy' between herself and Bernard and denies even more vehemently Chloë's assertion that her brother Gus is in love with her: 'That's a joke! ... How can you be so ridiculous?', even though Gus has brought her an apple, a token of his affection, which, like the apple of Eden, is especially suggestive (pp. 33-4). Indeed, Chloë seems to be Hannah's emotional and erotic conscience, for she earnestly asks, 'You've been deeply wounded in the past, haven't you, Hannah?' (p. 57).

When Bernard makes a pass at Hannah, she does not succumb:

Bernard: ... Why don't you come?
Hannah: Where?
Bernard: With me.
Hannah: To London? What for?
Bernard: What for.
Hannah: Oh, your lecture.
Bernard: No, no, bugger that. Sex.
Hannah: Oh ... No. Thanks ... (*then, protesting*) Bernard!

Bernard: You should try it. It's very underrated.
Hannah: Nothing against it.
Bernard: Yes, you have. You should let yourself go a bit (p. 63, emphasis original).

The rebuffed Bernard then makes it clear that while Hannah may not find him attractive, the young Chloë does.

Hannah: Bernard! – you haven't seduced that girl?
Bernard: Seduced her? Every time I turned round she was up a library ladder. In the end I gave in. That reminds me – I spotted something between her legs that made me think of you. (*He instantly receives a sharp stinging slap on the face but manages to remain completely unperturbed by it* ...) (p. 64).

Even at the end of the play, Hannah reluctantly joins Gus in the dance. As if to counter the saucy opening line ('What is carnal embrace?'), Hannah delivers the last line: 'Oh, dear, I don't really ...'.

One is hard pressed to find a redeeming woman in the play. The Lady Croom, who fancies Lord Byron, finally succumbs to Septimus' attentions and invites him to her room for an assignation. Years later, she has an amorous encounter off-stage with Count Zelinsky at the piano in the next room, as the stage directions make clear: '*The piano music becomes rapidly more passionate, and then breaks off suddenly in mid-phrase. There is an expressive silence next door which makes* Septimus *raise his eyes ... A few moments later* Lady Croom *enters from the music room, seeming surprised and slightly flustered*' (p. 81). Only Thomasina, it seems, remains pure, but even so her relationship with Septimus is tinged with sexuality that engages the male fantasy of intercourse with a mother and her daughter. *Arcadia* is a feminist's nightmare.

What reasons could Stoppard have for writing such women? The genre demands it; wayward sexuality is the stuff of drawing-room comedy. The plot demands it; *Arcadia* is driven by Hannah's discovery that Bernard is wrong. The temporal setting demands it; the Victorian era was characterized by sexual repression and the aberrations that so much repression causes. Could he have written a less licentious Mrs Chater, a less corrupted Lady Croom, a more sensible Chloë, or a more stable Hannah, without compromising the genre, plot, or temporal setting? Perhaps *Arcadia* is a starting point; for a playwright whose first critical success had no women, *Arcadia* represents a substantial improvement. Perhaps in future works, female characters will continue to evolve. Hannah's intelligence and Thomasina's gifted perceptions are a far cry from the objectified women of *Jumpers* and *Travesties*; however, it seems as though these two smart women cannot occupy the same place at the same time. When Hannah and Thomasina 'meet' in the final seventh scene, both appear to lose their senses under the spell of the men on stage.

VI

If one is looking for a strong female character, *The Invention of Love* will disappoint. In this cast of twenty-three characters, there is only one woman, Housman's sister Kate. An imagined and terribly unfortunate Miss Burton, confused for Miss Frobisher, bears the professor's humiliation ('Oh dear, I hope it is not I who have made you cry', p. 48) in silence. Jackson's girlfriend Rosa is mentioned briefly but never appears, and Housman and Jackson have a hard time finding a suitable poem for her from among the Roman elegies, for the poems either 'make her out to be a harlot' or 'make her out to be, well, *your* harlot' (p. 74). *The Invention of Love* is a man's play, and, in all fairness, Stoppard 'does' men extremely well.

In this two-act play, the leading man is 'a minor poet who lived like a hermit and was staggeringly rude' (Fleming 2001, 224). Yet Stoppard does not scruple to provide a setting in which the pigeon can appear as a dove. The curtain rises to the aged Housman (AEH) dreaming he is on the bank of the river Styx, watching for the approach of the ferryman Charon. Charon greets AEH and says they are to wait for a second passenger:

AEH: ... Are you sure?
Charon: A poet and a scholar is what I was told.
AEH: I think that must be me.
Charon: Both of them?
AEH: I'm afraid so.
Charon: It sounded like two different people (p. 2).

140

5. The Invention of Gardens

The twinning is characteristically Stoppard. And throughout the play, Housman is two different people; poet and scholar, young man and old, pitiable victim of prejudice and at the same time maddeningly arrogant misanthrope (see Mendelsohn, August 2000).

The play consists of a series of dream-recollections of Housman's youth, as a student at Oxford, and as a clerk in the patent office after he inexplicably failed his final examinations and left college, the years from 1877 to 1885. In the first act, the river connects several dream-like sequences that take place along its banks. Oxford dons Pater, Ruskin, Jowett, and Ellis play a game of croquet during which they discuss the value of a classical education and the immorality of homosexuality. Housman and his chum Pollard cheer on the athletic Moses Jackson in a race. The shy and reserved Housman is in love with Jackson, although his unrequited affection is not articulated until the next act.

The second act focuses on Housman's post-Oxford life. He works at the patent office and shares a flat with Jackson, who has fallen in love with the woman he will marry. Interwoven with these memories from Housman's youth are scenes about the enactment of the Criminal Law Amendment and the Labouchere Amendment, which made homosexual activity a crime, and Oscar Wilde's conviction and prison sentence for sodomy charges. In a painfully poignant scene that is the climax of the plot, Housman's affections are revealed to a surprised Jackson: 'How could I know? You seem just like ... you know, normal. You're not one of those Aesthete types or anything – (*angrily*) how could I know?!' (p. 77). Yet Jackson forgives Housman. Stage lighting brings up AEH quoting lines from his caustic critical editions in which he scathingly insults other scholars, while a selection committee reviews his application for a professorship. Meanwhile, the celebrated arrest of Oscar Wilde is in the newspapers.

On the bank of the river, AEH meets up with an old colleague from the patent office, Chamberlain, who knows his poetry well, but garbles it, much to AEH's annoyance, as if to recreate for the audience the process by which Latin poetry has been conveyed and (hopelessly?) garbled by the ages. Chamberlain tells AEH that he and his brother have formed a 'sort of secret society' and they discuss what they should call themselves. ' "Homosexuals" has been suggested' (p. 91).

AEH finally encounters Wilde himself, arguably his foil in the play,

141

who articulates in conclusion the 'invention of love': 'but before Plato could describe love, the loved one had to be invented. We would never love anybody if we could see past our invention' (p. 95). AEH has one last exchange with his younger self before the end – 'But now I really do have to go' (p. 102).

In the end, the garden is a locus of mutability, a place for transgression and transformation. Its principles of growth and decay, weeding and pruning, selection and exclusion make it a fertile metaphor for empire, politics, representation, and conversion. It seems only fitting, if paradoxically so, that the garden discharge one last duty as a metaphor for Classics, a metaphor subtly adumbrated by Stoppard throughout *The Invention of Love*.

As the companion to *Arcadia*, it would make sense that gardens also figure in *The Invention of Love*. In the first place, there are the explicit references to gardens in the play. When Housman is working at the patent office and continuing his scholarly activities, he tries to defend his occupation to his friend Pollard:

> Propertius looked to me like a garden gone to wilderness, and not a very interesting garden either, but what an opportunity! – it was begging to be put back in order. Better still, various nincompoops thought they had already done it … hacking about, to make room for their dandelions (p. 69).

The elder AEH returns to this very criticism when the selection committee reviews his application:

> When I with some thought and some pains have got this rather uninteresting garden into decent order, here is Dr Postgate hacking at the fence in a spirited attempt to re-establish chaos amongst Propertius manuscripts (p. 81).

Thus both the young and the old Housman refer to textual criticism as a kind of gardening. The image takes on a less caustic, more haunting tone toward the end of the play, when AEH, in dialogue with Housman, explains that Gallus, not Propertius, was the first Roman elegist, and that, though the poems of Gallus have perished, still 'his memory [is] alive in a garden' (p. 98).

Secondly, throughout the play there are references to unfulfilled desire and the longing for something unattainable, something forever lost. Jamaica Kincaid distils Elkin's dictum, that gardens are 'open-ended sites of desire:'

> I shall never have the garden I have in my mind, but that for me is the joy of it; certain things can never be realized and so all the more reason to attempt them. A garden, no matter how good it is, must never completely satisfy. The world as we know it, after all, began in a very good garden, a completely satisfying garden – Paradise – but after a while the owner and the occupants wanted more (Kincaid 1999, 220).

As the pastoral ideal longs for a lost way of life, so the garden is incapable of satisfying that longing. With its perpetual state of becoming, the garden cannot fulfil; it can only hold out a promise. In the words of the gnomic Ian Hamilton Finlay, 'Gardens are always for *next* year.'

The Invention of Love is punctuated by a futile longing for knowledge that can never be possessed. In the opening scene, AEH and Charon converse about the ferryman's role in Aristophanes' *Frogs*. Charon reminisces about an even better play, Aeschylus' *Myrmidones*. AEH becomes very excited at the prospect of Charon reciting lines of this lost play, but he is sorely frustrated when the ferryman only repeats the extant fragments. Twice in the play, both AEH and Housman repeat the line, 'That's what they all wanted to know' (pp. 45, 50), when asked why he failed his final exams in May 1881, an unsolved mystery to this day. Twice in the play the young Housman asks, 'What do I want?' (pp. 64, 72), in a question that articulates not only desire, but the ignorance of that desire. Then, as if to define the 'field' of classics, Housman compares the extant classics to

> ... a cornfield after the reaping. Laid flat to stubble, and here and there, unaccountably, miraculously spared, a few stalks still upright. Why those? There is no reason. Ovid's Medea, the Thyestes of Varius ... the lost Aeschylus trilogy of the Trojan war ... gathered to oblivion in *sheaves*, along with hundreds of Greek and Roman authors known only for fragments or their names

143

alone – and here and there a cornstalk, a thistle, a poppy, still standing ... (pp. 71-2).

Like Thomasina's lament for the library at Alexandria in *Arcadia*, so Housman laments the irrecoverable. The entire enterprise of textual criticism is predicated on finding a lost reading. The classics arouse desire because they do not exist, they have to be invented, in the etymological sense of the word (from *invenire*, to come upon): they have to be found. This desire for something that has to be found, discovered (indeed, uncovered, in the original sense of the word), and invented, characterizes the garden. Gardens are completely human constructs that are the result of a desire for nature in a particular way, or a desire for food in a particular way, and not the way it is simply given. Gardens are constructed because they fill a void, an absence which arouses a desire. The human condition can be measured by the extent to which one will go to fill that void.

Stoppard's metaphors of the garden in *The Invention of Love* are so effective because classics appeal in the same way gardens do. Both are the absent objects of desire. Both confer a sense of privileged inclusion to those who enter. Both can only be maintained by scrupulous up-keep. Both are capable of stripping away the powers of time and space. Both embody the sacred and the profane. Neither can be completely recovered or recreated. Neither completely satisfies.

Stoppard's biographer Ira Nadel asks, 'Why did Stoppard bother to respond to Mendelsohn?' (2002, 517). For a classicist, however, the more pressing question is, Why did Mendelsohn continue to respond to Stoppard? Because *The Invention of Love* puts centre-stage the debate that has plagued classics for some time, namely, the usefulness of *Altertumswissenschaft*. Utility is twice defended by Jowett, who concludes, 'If you cannot write Latin and Greek verse how can you hope to be of any use in the world?' (pp. 23-4). The defence continues in a conversation between Housman and AEH, as the elder instructs the younger on the purpose of textual criticism: 'A small victory over ignorance and error. A scrap of knowledge to add to our stock' (p. 38). It would seem that Jackson opens the debate most stridently: 'What gets *my* goat, actually, if you want to know, is that the fellow [Richard Bentley] isn't worth the fuss, none of them are – I mean, what *use* is he to anyone?' (p. 55, emphasis original); however, although the immediate antecedent of 'the fellow' is presumably Bentley, in fact Jackson is upset by Oscar Wilde. Conflict is averted, and Housman never gets to defend his 'science' to Jackson (himself a scientist). By the time the utility of textual criticism is questioned again, Chamberlain reduces it to a mere coin-toss (p. 68). We are left with an unsatisfactory defence of the usefulness of textual criticism, and by metonymy, classics.

Although Stoppard uses the debate for theatrical purposes in a play with many themes beyond classics, he nevertheless materializes a perception of the futility of textual criticism and thereby steps precipitously into a deep rift that bisects classics (for a thought-provoking examination of the state of classics in American education, see Pearcy 2005). A recent example of this scholarly divide is provided by a short article on Statius *Silvae* 2.6.38-43 written by the late Shackleton Bailey, whose flair for affrontery is reminiscent of Housman's: 'That Baehrens should miss the point is no surprise, but that two of Statius' best critics ... should each spend pages in a similar fog, leaves me agasp' (2001-2, 177). He closes his brief note, which he has titled, 'Tí deî me choreúein;' or 'Why should I dance?' with a series of questions, prompted by the rumour that a leading classics journal has decided not to publish critical notes any longer:

(a) Do matters of textual and verbal interpretation, what classical authors wrote and what they meant, still have a place in classical philology? (b) Are all such questions canonically settled for the rest of time? (c) Does a competent readership still exist for contributions of this nature? At all events it has suggested my heading – not that my dancing days are likely to be long anyway (2001-2, 177-8).

How interesting that Shackleton Bailey should fashion his futility in terms of one of Greek drama's most memorable metatheatrical moments. In Sophocles' *Oedipus the King*, the chorus of Theban elders asks, if people act without fear of justice or reverence for the gods, then 'Why should we join in the sacred dance?' As the Sophoclean chorus seeks to distance itself from profanity, so one could easily see Stoppard's AEH asking the same question: Why should I participate in this vain drama? Why should I dance? As the science of textual criticism is on the decline, so gardening is no longer practised as a fine art.

145

'Major artists do not make statements in this medium', according to Ross, 'and our sense of gardening's kinship to painting and poetry has been lost' (1998, 202). What resemblance do the environmental installations of Alan Sonfist or Christo & Jeanne-Claude (see Ross 1998, 208-19) bear to the formal gardens of Versailles – or the pleasure gardens of ancient Rome? What resemblance do the contributions to the Classical Inter/Faces series bear to the editions of Propertius collated by the contentious scholar-scientists of the nineteenth and early twentieth century? In short, to conclude my comparison, both gardens and classics have experienced – and survived – the profound ontological transformations wrought in part by the condition of postmodernity.

Such profound transformations trigger the two disparate (and sometimes desperate) responses of reactionaries on the one hand, and revolutionaries on the other. One could, like Stoppard's Housman, cling to a science whose utility was never proven satisfactorily and lament the loss or curse the change. On the other hand, one could recklessly ignore the contributions of textual critics, and in ignorance of the science, condemn its uselessness. As our society becomes not only increasingly a-historical, but distressingly anti-historical, to the point of miso-historical, if I may coin a term, the latter response is perhaps all too familiar. But to preserve the integrity – the wholeness – of classics is to accept its past, to know its purpose in the present, and to offer it freely – no strings attached – to future generations.

Bibliography

Abrioux, Y. (1985) *Ian Hamilton Finlay: A Visual Primer* (Edinburgh).

Agamben, G. (1999) *Remnants of Auschwitz: The Witness and the Archive*, translated by D. Heller-Roazen (New York).

Althusser, L. (1971) *Lenin and Philosophy and Other Essays*, translated by B. Brewster (New York and London).

Anderson, W.S. (1982) *Essays on Roman Satire* (Princeton).

Archer, L.J., Fischler, S., and Wyke, M., eds (1994) *Women in Ancient Societies: An Illusion of the Night* (New York).

Ash, R. (1999) *Ordering Anarchy: Armies and Leaders in Tacitus' Histories* (Ann Arbor).

Attridge, D. (2004) *J. M. Coetzee and the Ethics of Reading: Literature in the Event* (Chicago).

Baldwin, B. (1963) 'Columella's Sources and How he Used Them', *Latomus* 22: 785-91.

Bann, S. (1981) 'A Description of Stonypath', *Journal of Garden History* 1.2: 113-44.

Barchiesi, A. (2001) 'Horace and Iambos: The Poet as Literary Historian', in A. Cavarzere, A. Aloni, and A. Barchiesi, eds, *Iambic Ideas: Essays on a Poetic Tradition from Archaic Greece to the late Roman Empire* (Lanham, MD) 141-63.

Barthes, R. (1972) *Mythologies*, translated by A. Lavers (New York).

—— (1976) *Sade/Fourier/Loyola*, translated by R. Miller (New York).

Beard, M. (1998) 'Imaginary *Horti*: Or Up the Garden Path', in M. Cima and E. LaRocca, eds, *Horti Romani* (Rome) 23-32.

Beck, T.E. (2002) 'Gardens as a "Third Nature": The Ancient Roots of a Renaissance Idea', *Studies in the History of Gardens and Designed Landscapes* 22: 327-34.

Bidart, F. (1997) *Desire* (New York).

Bigelow, J. (1859) *Nature in Disease: illustrated in various discourses and essays. To which are added miscellaneous writings, chiefly on medical subjects* (New York).

Boatwright, M.T. (1998) 'Luxuriant Gardens and Extravagant Women: The

Horti of Rome between Republic and Empire', in M. Cima and E. LaRocca, eds, *Horti Romani* (Rome) 71-82.

Bodel, J. (1986 [1994]) 'Graveyards and Groves: A Study of the *Lex Lucerina*', *American Journal of Ancient History* 11: 1-133.

Bowe, P. (2004) *Gardens of the Roman World* (Los Angeles).

Bowersock, G.W. (1971) 'A Date in the Eighth *Eclogue*', *Harvard Studies in Classical Philology* 75: 73-80.

—— (1978) 'The Addressee of the Eighth *Eclogue*: A Response', *Harvard Studies in Classical Philology* 82: 201-2.

Braund, S. (1989) 'City and Country in Roman Satire', in S. Braund, ed., *Satire and Society in Ancient Rome* (Exeter) 23-47.

—— (1992) *Roman Verse Satire*. Oxford.

—— (2002) *Latin Literature* (London and New York).

Braund, S., and James, P. 1998. '*Quasi Homo*: Distortion and Contortion in Seneca's *Apocolocyntosis*', *Arethusa* 31: 285-311.

Bréguet, E. (1969) '*Urbi et orbi*: Un cliché et un thème', in J. Bibauw, ed., *Hommages à Marcel Renard* vol. 1, *Collection Latomus* vol. 101 (Brussels) 140-52.

Broise, H., and Jolivet, V. (1985) 'Recherches sur les Jardins de Lucullus', in *L'Urbs: Espace Urbain et Histoire (Ier siècle av. J.-C.-IIIe siècle ap. J.-C.)* (Paris and Rome) 747-61.

Brown, P. (2000) *Augustine of Hippo: A Biography*. New Edition with an Epilogue (Berkeley and Los Angeles).

Brown, P.M. (1993) *Horace: Satires I* (Warminster).

Carroll, M. (2003) *Earthly Paradises: Ancient Gardens in History and Archaeology* (London).

Carroll-Spillecke, M. (1992) 'The Gardens of Greece from Homeric to Roman Times', *Journal of Garden History* 12: 84-101.

Chassignet, M. (2003) 'La Naissance de l'Autobiographie à Rome: *Laus sui ou Apologia de Vita sua?*', *Revue des Études Latines* 81: 65-78.

Ciarallo, A. (2000) *Gardens of Pompeii*, translated by L.-A. Touchette (Rome).

Clark, G. (1995) *Augustine Confessions Books I-IV* (Cambridge).

Clausen, W. (1972) 'On the Date of the First *Eclogue*', *Harvard Studies in Classical Philology* 76: 201-5.

Coetzee, J.M. (1983) *Life & Times of Michael K* (London).

—— (1984) *Truth in Autobiography*. Inaugural Lecture (Cape Town).

—— (2004) *Lecture and Speech of Acceptance Upon the Award of the Nobel Prize in Literature, Delivered in Stockholm in December 2003* (New York).

Coffey, M. (1976) *Roman Satire* (London).

Bibliography

Colin, J. (1956) 'Les Vendanges Dionysiaques et la Légende de Messaline (48 ap. J.-C.): Tacite, *Annales*, XI, 25-38', *Les Études Classiques* 24: 25-39.

Conan, M. (1986) 'Nature into Art: Gardens and Landscapes in the Everyday Life of Ancient Rome', *Journal of Garden History* 6: 348-56.

Copley, F. (1956) *Exclusus Amator: A Study in Latin Love Poetry* (Baltimore).

Corbier, M. (1995) 'Male Power and Legitimacy through Women: The *Domus Augusta* under the Julio-Claudians', in R. Hawley and B. Levick, eds, *Women in Antiquity: New Assessments* (London and New York) 178-93.

Cossarini, A. (1977) 'Aspetti di Virgilio in Columella', *Prometheus* 3: 225-40.

Courcelle, P. (1950) *Recherches sur les Confessions de Saint Augustin* (Paris).

——— (1963) *Les Confessions de Saint Augustin dans la Tradition Littéraire: Antécédents et Postérité* (Paris).

Courtney, E. (1993) *The Fragmentary Latin Poets* (Oxford).

Crozier, M. (1999) 'After the Garden?', *The South Atlantic Quarterly* 98: 625-31.

Delaney, P. (2001) 'Exit Tomáš Straüssler, enter Sir Tom Stoppard', In K.E. Kelly, ed., *The Cambridge Companion to Tom Stoppard* (Cambridge) 25-37.

Dickison, S. (1977) 'Claudius: *Saturnalicius Princeps*', *Latomus* 36: 634-47.

Doll, M.A. (1993) 'Stoppard's Theatre of Unknowing', in J. Acheson, ed., *British and Irish Drama since 1960* (New York) 117-29.

Dovey, T. (1988) *The Novels of J M Coetzee: Lacanian Allegories* (Cape Town).

DuQuesnay, I. (1984) 'Horace and Maecenas: The Propaganda Value of *Sermones* I', in A.J. Woodman and D. West, eds, *Poetry and Politics in the Age of Augustus* (Cambridge) 19-58.

Durrant, S. (2004) *Postcolonial Narrative and the Work of Mourning: J.M. Coetzee, Wilson Harris, and Toni Morrison* (Albany).

Edwards, C. (1993) *The Politics of Immorality in Ancient Rome* (Cambridge).

——— (1997) 'Unspeakable Professions: Public Performance and Prostitution in Ancient Rome,' in J.P. Hallett and M.B. Skinner, eds, *Roman Sexualities* (Princeton) 66-95.

Edwards, P. (2001) 'Science in *Hapgood* and *Arcadia*', in K.E. Kelly, ed., *The Cambridge Companion to Tom Stoppard* (Cambridge) 171-84.

Ehrhardt, C. (1978) 'Messalina and the Succession to Claudius', *Antichthon* 12: 51-71.

Elkins, J. (1993) 'On the Conceptual Analysis of Gardens', *Journal of Garden History* 13: 189-98.

Ernout, A., and Meillet, A. (1959) *Dictionnaire Étymologique de la Langue Latine: Histoire des Mots*. 4th edn (Paris).

Esler, C.C. (1989) 'Horace's Old Girls: Evolution of a Topos', in T.M. Falkner and J. de Luce, eds, *Old Age in Greek and Latin Literature* (Albany) 172-82.

Bibliography

Eyres, P. (2000) 'Ian Hamilton Finlay and the Cultural Poetics of Neo-Classical Gardening', *Garden History* 28.1: 152-66.

―――― (2006) 'Planting for Perpetuity,' *Historic Gardens Review* 16: 22-7.

Farrar, L. (1998) *Ancient Roman Gardens* (Stroud).

Feeney, D. (1991) *The Gods in Epic: Poets and Critics of the Classical Tradition* (Oxford).

Ferrari, L. (1970) 'The Pear-Theft in Augustine's *Confessions*', *Revue des Études Augustiniennes* 16: 233-42.

―――― (1979) 'The Arboreal Polarisation in Augustine's *Confessions*', *Revue des Études Augustiniennes* 25: 35-46.

―――― (1984) *The Conversions of Saint Augustine* (Villanova).

―――― (1989) 'Saint Augustine's Conversion Scene: The End of a Modern Debate?', *Studia Patristica* 22: 235-50.

―――― (2003) 'Book 8: Science and the Fictional Conversion Scene', In K. Paffenroth and R.P. Kennedy, eds, *A Reader's Companion to Augustine's Confessions* (Louisville and London) 127-36.

Fitzgerald, W. (1988) 'Power and Impotence in Horace's *Epodes*', *Ramus* 17: 176-91.

Fleming, J.P. (2001) *Stoppard's Theatre: Finding Order amid Chaos* (Austin).

Forché, C. (1994) *The Angel of History* (New York).

Forster, E.S. (1950) 'Columella and His Latin Treatise on Agriculture', *Greece and Rome* 19: 123-8.

Foucault, M. (1977) *Language, Counter-Memory, Practice: Selected Essays and Interviews*, translated by D. Bouchard and S. Simon (Ithaca).

―――― (1986) 'Of Other Spaces', translated by J. Miskowiec. *Diacritics* 16: 22-7.

Fraenkel, E. (1957) *Horace* (Oxford).

Francis, M., and Hester, R.T., eds (1990) *The Meaning of Gardens* (Cambridge, MA).

Freudenburg, K. (2001) *Satires of Rome: Threatening Poses from Lucilius to Juvenal* (Cambridge).

Gillanders, R. (1998) *Little Sparta. Detached Sentences, Ian Hamilton Finlay; afterward, Alec Finlay* (Edinburgh).

Ginsburg, J. (2006) *Representing Agrippina: Constructions of Female Power in the Early Roman Empire* (Oxford).

Gordimer, N. (1998) 'The Idea of Gardening: *Life and Times of Michael K* by J.M. Coetzee (Review)', in S. Kossew, ed., *Critical Essays on J.M. Coetzee* (New York) 139-44.

Gowers, E. (2000) 'Vegetable Love: Virgil, Columella, and Garden Poetry', *Ramus* 29: 127-48.

Griffin, J. (1984) 'Augustus and the Poets: "Caesar qui cogere posset" ', in F. Millar and E. Segal, eds, *Caesar Augustus: Seven Aspects* (Oxford) 189-218.

Bibliography

—— (1993) 'Horace in the Thirties', in N. Rudd, ed., *Horace 2000: A Celebration: Essays for the Bimillennium* (London) 1-22.

Griffin, M. (1990) 'Claudius in Tacitus', *Classical Quarterly* 40: 482-501.

Grimal, P. (1984) *Les Jardins Romains*. 3rd edn (Paris).

Gusdorf, G. (1980) 'Conditions and Limits of Autobiography', in J. Olney, ed., *Autobiography: Essays Theoretical and Critical* (Princeton) 28-48.

Gussow, M. (1995) *Conversations with Stoppard* (New York).

Habinek, T. (1998) *The Politics of Latin Literature: Writing, Identity, and Empire in Ancient Rome* (Princeton).

Hallett, J.P. (1981) '*Pepedi/diffissa nate ficus*: Priapic Revenge in Horace *Satires* 1.8', *Rheinisches Museum für Philologie* 124: 341-7.

Halperin, D. (1983) *Before Pastoral: Theocritus and the Ancient Tradition of Bucolic Poetry* (New Haven and London).

—— (1990) 'Pastoral Violence in the *Georgics*: Commentary on Ross', *Arethusa* 23: 77-93.

Harrison, S. (2001) 'Some Generic Problems in Horace's *Epodes*: Or, On (Not) Being Archilochus', in A. Aloni, A. Cavarzere, and A. Barchiesi, eds, *Iambic Ideas: Essays on a Poetic Tradition from Archaic Greece to the late Roman Empire* (Lanham, MD) 165-86.

Harvey, D. (1990) *The Condition of Postmodernity: An Enquiry into the Origins of Cultural Change* (Oxford).

Hedrick, C.W. (2000) *History and Silence: Purge and Rehabilitation of Memory in Late Antiquity* (Austin).

Heider, S.D. (1993) 'The Timeless Ecstasy of Michael K', in P. Fletcher, ed., *Black/White Writing: Essays on South African Literature* (Cranbury, NJ) 83-98.

Helphand, K. (1997) 'Defiant Gardens', *Journal of Garden History* 17: 101-21.

Henderson, J. (2002) 'Columella's Living Hedge: The Roman Gardening Book', *Journal of Roman Studies* 92: 110-33.

—— (2004) *HORTUS: The Roman Book of Gardening* (London).

Henrichs, A. (1978) 'Greek Maenadism from Olympias to Messalina', *Harvard Studies in Classical Philology* 82: 121-60.

Hopkins, K. (1983) *Death and Renewal* (Cambridge).

Hunt, J.D. (1991) 'The Garden as Cultural Object', in S. Wrede and W.H. Adams, eds, *Denatured Visions: Landscape and Culture in the Twentieth Century* (New York) 19-32.

—— (1997) 'The Garden as Virtual Reality', in M. Kohler, ed., *Das künstliche Paradies* (Worms am Rhein) 5-14.

—— (1999) 'Approaches (New and Old) to Garden History', in M. Conan, ed., *Perspectives on Garden Histories* (Washington, DC) 77-90.

—— (2004) *The Afterlife of Gardens* (Philadelphia).

Bibliography

Hunter, J. (2000) *Tom Stoppard: Rosencrantz and Guildenstern are Dead, Jumpers, Travesties, Arcadia* (London).

Huxley, A. (1978) *An Illustrated History of Gardening* (New York).

JanMohamed, A.R. (1983) *Manichean Aesthetics: The Politics of Literature in Colonial Africa* (Amherst).

Jashemski, W.F. (1979) *The Gardens of Pompeii, Herculaneum, and the Villas Destroyed by Vesuvius* (New Rochelle, New York).

Jashemski, W.F., and Meyer, F.G., eds (2002) *The Natural History of Pompeii* (Cambridge).

Johnson, W.R. (2004) 'A Secret Garden: *Georgics* 4.116-148', in D. Armstrong, M. Skinner, and P. Johnson, eds, *Vergil, Philodemus and the Augustans* (Austin) 75-83.

Joshel, S. (1997) 'Female Desire and the Discourse of Empire: Tacitus's Messalina', in J. Hallett and M. Skinner, eds, *Roman Sexualities* (Princeton) 221-54.

Kaster, G. (1974) *Die Gärten des Lucullus: Entwicklung und Bedeutung der Bebauung des Pincio-Hügels in Rom* (Munich).

Keaveney, A. (1992) *Lucullus: A Life* (London and New York).

Keitel, E. (1978) 'The Role of Parthia and Armenia in Tacitus *Annals* 11 and 12', *American Journal of Philology* 99: 462-73.

Kiernan, V.G. (1999) *Horace: Poetics and Politics* (New York).

Kincaid, J. (1999) *My Garden (Book):* (New York).

Lawson, J. (1950) 'The Roman Garden', *Greece and Rome* 19: 97-105.

Leach, E.W. (1978) 'Vergil, Horace, Tibullus: Three Collections of Ten', *Ramus* 7: 79-105.

—— (1984) 'Transformations in the *Georgics*: Vergil's Italy and Varro's', in *Atti del Convegno mondiale scientifico di studi su Virgilio* (Milan) 85-108.

Lejay, P. (1966) *Oeuvres d'Horace: Satires* (Hildesheim).

Leon, E. (1948) 'The *Imbecillitas* of the Emperor Claudius', *Transactions and Proceedings of the American Philological Association* 79: 79-86.

Levick, B. (1990) *Claudius* (New Haven and London).

Lyne, R.O.A.M. (1995) *Horace: Behind the Public Poetry* (New Haven and London).

MacCormack, S. (1998) *The Shadows of Poetry: Vergil in the Mind of Augustine* (Berkeley).

Mankin, D., ed. (1995) *Horace Epodes* (Cambridge).

Manning, C.E. (1970) 'Canidia in the *Epodes* of Horace', *Mnemosyne* 23: 393-401.

Mansbach, S.A. (1982) 'An Earthwork of Surprise: The 18th-Century Ha-Ha', *Art Journal* 42: 217-21.

Marais, M. (2001) 'Literature and the Labour of Negation: J.M. Coetzee's

Bibliography

Life & Times of Michael K', *Journal of Commonwealth Literature* 36: 107-25.

Marshall, L.B. (1918) *L'Horticulture Antique et le Poème de Columelle (De re rustica, livre X)* (Paris and London).

Martin, R. (1981) *Tacitus* (Bristol).

Martindale, C. (1993) *Redeeming the Text: Latin Poetry and the Hermeneutics of Reception* (Cambridge).

McGann, M.J. (1973) 'The Three Worlds of Horace's *Satires*', in C.D.N. Costa, ed., *Horace* (London) 59-93.

Mehl, A. (1974) *Tacitus über Kaiser Claudius: die Ereignisse am Hof* (Munich).

Meise, E. (1969) *Untersuchungen zur Geschichte der Julisch-Claudischen Dynastie* (Munich).

Mellor, R. (1993) *Tacitus* (London).

Mendelsohn, D. (2000) 'The Tale of Two Housmans', *New York Review of Books*, 10 August, 58-65.

Merivale, P. (1996) 'Audible Palimpsests: Coetzee's Kafka', in G. Huggan and S. Watson, eds, *Critical Perspectives on J.M. Coetzee* (New York) 152-67.

Miller, P.A. (1998) 'The Bodily Grotesque in Roman Satire: Images of Sterility', *Arethusa* 31: 257-83.

Milnor, K. (2005) *Gender, Domesticity, and the Age of Augustus: Inventing Private Life* (Oxford).

Morford, M. (1987) 'The Stoic Garden', *Journal of Garden History* 7: 151-75.

Morgan, E. (1995) 'Finlay in the 70s and 80s', in A. Finlay, ed. *Wood Notes Wild: Essays on the Poetry and Art of Ian Hamilton Finlay* (Edinburgh) 137-47.

Nadel, I. (2002) *Tom Stoppard: A Life* (New York).

Newman, J.K. (1998) 'Iambe/Iambos and the Rape of a Genre: A Horatian Sidelight', *Illinois Classical Studies* 23: 101-20.

Nisbet, R.G.M. (1984) 'Horace's *Epodes* and History', in A.J. Woodman and D. West, eds, *Poetry and Politics in the Age of Augustus* (Cambridge) 1-18.

Nisbet, R.G.M., and Hubbard, M. (1970) *A Commentary on Horace: Odes Book 1* (Oxford).

Noè, E. (2002) *Il Progetto di Columella: Profilo sociale, economico, culturale* (Como).

O'Donnell, J.J. (1992) *The Confessions of Augustine: An Electronic Edition* (Oxford) http://ccat.sas.upenn.edu/jod/augustine.html.

———— (2005) *Augustine: A New Biography* (New York).

O'Meara, J.J. (1965) *The Young Augustine: The Growth of St. Augustine's Mind up to his Conversion* (New York).

Oliensis, E. (1991) 'Canidia, Canicula, and the Decorum of Horace's *Epodes*', *Arethusa* 24: 107-38.

———— (1998) *Horace and the Rhetoric of Authority* (Cambridge).

Bibliography

Osborne, R. (1992) 'Classical Greek Gardens: Between Farm and Paradise', In J.D. Hunt, ed., *Garden History: Issues, Approaches, Methods* (Washington, DC) 373-91.

Osgood, J.W. (2006) *Caesar's Legacy: Civil War and the Emergence of the Roman Empire* (Cambridge).

Parker, W.H. (1988) *Priapea: Poems for a Phallic God* (London).

—— (1998) 'Loyal Slaves and Loyal Wives: The Crisis of the Outsider-Within and Roman *Exemplum* Literature', in S. Joshel and S. Murnaghan, eds, *Women and Slaves in Greco-Roman Culture: Differential Equations* (New York) 152-73.

Patrizio, A. (1999) *Contemporary Sculpture in Scotland* (Sydney).

Pearcy, L.T. (2005) *The Grammar of Our Civility: Classical Education in America* (Waco, TX).

Pugh, S. (1988) *Garden – Nature – Language* (Manchester).

Purcell, N. (1987) 'Town in Country and Country in Town', in E.B. MacDougall, ed., *Ancient Roman Villa Gardens* (Washington, DC) 187-203.

—— (1987a) 'Tomb and Suburb', in H. von Hesberg and P. Zanker, eds, *Römische Gräberstraßen: Selbstdarstellung, Status, Standard* (Munich) 25-41.

Putnam, M. (1972) 'Horace and Tibullus', *Classical Philology* 67: 81-8.

Radke, G. (1965) *Die Götter Altitaliens* (Munster).

Reay, B. (2005) 'Agriculture, Writing, and Cato's Aristocratic Self-Fashioning', *Classical Antiquity* 24: 331-61.

Rehm, R. (2003) *Radical Theatre: Greek Tragedy and the Modern World* (London).

Richlin, A. (1984) 'Invective against Women in Roman Satire', *Arethusa* 17: 67-80.

—— (1992) *The Garden of Priapus: Sexuality and Aggression in Roman Humor* revised edn (Oxford).

Ross, S. (1998) *What Gardens Mean* (Chicago).

Rudd, N. (1966) *The Satires of Horace* (Cambridge).

Scobie, S. (1995) 'Models of Order,' in A. Finlay, ed., *Wood Notes Wild: Essays on the Poetry and Art of Ian Hamilton Finlay* (Edinburgh) 177-205.

Shackleton Bailey, D.R. (2001-2) 'Tí deî me choreúein;', *Classical Journal* 97: 177-8.

Sheeler, J. (2003) *Little Sparta: The Garden of Ian Hamilton Finlay* (London).

Sinclair, P. (1995) *Tacitus the Sententious Historian* (University Park, PA).

Skinner, M.B. (1997) '*Quod multo fit aliter in Graecia*', in J.P. Hallett and M.B. Skinner, eds, *Roman Sexualities* (Princeton) 3-25.

Stoppard, T. 1993. *Arcadia* (London).

—— (1997) *The Invention of Love* (New York).

Stoppard, T., and Mendelsohn, D. (2000) ' "The Invention of Love": An Exchange', *New York Review of Books*, 21 September, 103-5.

154

Bibliography

—— (2000) 'On "The Invention of Love": Another Exchange', *New York Review*, 19 October, 64-5.

Syme, R. (1939) *The Roman Revolution* (Oxford).

—— (1970) *Ten Studies in Tacitus* (Oxford).

Tarrant, R.J. (1978) 'The Addressee of Virgil's Eighth *Eclogue*', *Harvard Studies in Classical Philology* 82: 197-9.

Thacker, C. (1979) *The History of Gardens* (Berkeley and Los Angeles).

Thomas, R.F. (1987) 'Prose into Poetry: Tradition and Meaning in Virgil's *Georgics*', *Harvard Studies in Classical Philology* 91: 229-60.

—— ed. (1988) *Virgil: Georgics*, vol. 1: Books I-II (Cambridge).

Valder, P. (2002) *Gardens in China* (Portland, OR).

van Erp-Houtepen, A. (1986) 'The Etymological Origin of the Garden', *Journal of Garden History* 6: 227-31.

van Rooy, C.A. 1973. ' "Imitatio" of Vergil, *Eclogues* in Horace, *Satires*, Book I', *Acta Classica* 16: 69-88.

Vessey, D. (1971) 'Thoughts on Tacitus' Portrayal of Claudius', *American Journal of Ancient History* 92: 385-409.

Wallace-Hadrill, A. (1998) '*Horti* and Hellenization', in M. Cima and E. LaRocca, eds, *Horti Romani* (Rome) 1-12.

Welch, T. (2001) '*Est locus uni cuique suus*: City and Status in Horace's *Satires* 1.8 and 1.9', *Classical Antiquity* 20: 165-92.

White, P. (1993) *Promised Verse: Poets in the Society of Augustan Rome* (Cambridge, MA).

Wiseman, T.P. (1995) *Remus: A Roman Myth* (Cambridge).

—— (1998) 'A Stroll on the Rampart', in M. Cima and E. LaRocca, eds, *Horti Romani* (Rome) 13-22.

Woodman, A.J. (1998) *Tacitus Reviewed* (Oxford).

Woodman, A.J., and Martin, R. (1996) *The Annals of Tacitus Book 3* (Cambridge).

Wortley, E. (1868) *Travels in the United States, etc. During 1849 and 1850* (New York).

Wyke, M. (2002) *The Roman Mistress: Ancient and Modern Representations* (Oxford).

Zetzel, J.E.G. (2002) 'Dreaming about Quirinus: Horace's *Satires* and the Development of Augustan Poetry', in A.J. Woodman and D. Feeney, eds, *Traditions and Contexts in the Poetry of Horace* (Cambridge) 38-52.

Zinman, T. 2001. '*Travesties, Night and Day, The Real Thing*', in K.E. Kelly, ed., *The Cambridge Companion to Tom Stoppard* (Cambridge) 120-35.

Index

Index